D1446880

Writing Production Music for TV

THE ROAD TO SUCCESS

by

Steve Barden

Foreword by Kevin Kiner

 To access audio, visit:
www.HalLeonard.com/MyLibrary
Enter Code
5283-8062-6759-1059

ISBN 978-1-57424-354-3

Copyright ©2017 CENTERSTREAM Publishing
P. O. Box 17878 - Anaheim Hills, CA 92817
email: centerstrm@aol.com • **web:** centerstream-usa.com

For Leanne

Table of Contents

CONTENTS

Foreword

I met Steve about 7 years ago after a music symposium for which I was a guest speaker. During my talk on scoring for TV and Film I brought along a small "rig" and demonstrated to the audience some of the tricks and secrets that I was currently using to score *CSI:Miami*. During the Q&A after my presentation I was barraged with the usual questions pertaining to how I got my start in the business, how I got to meet George Lucas and score *Star Wars: The Clone Wars*, etc. As usual I told my story, which is unique to only myself, just as is Steve's story, or Hans Zimmer's. I always preface the telling of my musical journey with something like, "well this is not going to be of much use to any of you if you are looking for the secret to becoming a successful composer. It's a story of work, luck, and above all an addiction to music".

As I was reading *Writing Production Music for TV - The Road to Success*, I was struck by the thought that THIS was what all of the eager musicians in the room were really looking for when they asked me how I had made a career out of composing. And as you can see from the table of contents, there is no one easy answer or paragraph or chapter that unveils the secrets to success in this field. However, much of what a prospective composer needs to know to get started, and more importantly to continue to grow a real career is contained in the following chapters. Schools do not teach this (much of the time because the professors couldn't make a living as a composer, that's why they became professors – sorry guys, but myself and many of my colleagues have been burned and I am weary of academia). This book is much needed and I'm privileged that Steve asked me to write this foreword.

One of my great loves is sharing musical insights with students. I have done and continue to do workshops and seminars whenever my schedule permits. What do you think my first question is to each bright-eyed talented potential composer I meet? I'll give you a hint, it's not "how would you voice Abmi7#11 for a section of 8 bassoons"...... Nope, my first question is "what DAW do you use?" My second question is "what sound libraries do you have, and what techniques do you use to make them sound like real orchestral instruments?" My third question is "how are your electronic music chops?" Invariably I get blank stares, and a few people raise their hands and say something like "I can use Finale, or Sibelius".... Gads, what is wrong with our music schools??!! 10% of the graduating class from Juilliard is making a living in music 2 years after having graduated! The Berklee College of Music is one of the rare exceptions to this pervasive lack of practical education, but that's about it.

Now I'm not saying that you don't need to learn harmony, counterpoint or any of the other marvelous facets of our craft. I myself try to read through at least one score from the masters every day (I seldom succeed, making a living intruding on lofty ambitions as it does, but it's a conceit that I refuse to let go of). What I am saying is if you really want to see royalty checks and feed your family as well as your passion, read this book, take the insights it has to offer to heart, and then get to know your DAW and sound libraries very, very well.

I will leave you with my four favorite quotes:

"Lesser artists borrow, great artists steal" – Igor Stravinsky
(Mozart stole from Haydn, who stole from.... We are building on the shoulders of giants)

"If it sounds good, it IS good" – Duke Ellington

"Genius is 99 percent perspiration and 1 percent inspiration" – Thomas Edison
(Widely used, but never more true than when pertaining to composing)

The last, and my favorite, comes from **Alan Silvestri** (*Back to the*

Future, *Forest Gump*, and about 100 more immortal classics). I was having lunch with him in 1983 and asked him what advice he had for me. He replied, *"Well, are you lucky?"*

After finishing chapter six of this book you will have taken your first step of many towards being "lucky".

Kevin Kiner
June 2017

Honored with multiple Emmy and Annie nominations as well as 14 BMI awards, Kevin Kiner is one of the most versatile and sought-after composers in Hollywood. Kevin's wide musical range has allowed him to take on such diverse projects as the Netflix hit, *Making a Murderer*, Disney's *Star Wars: Rebels*, AMC's hit series *Hell on Wheels*, CW's *Jane the Virgin*, and CBS's *CSI:Miami*. Kevin is currently co-composing with his two sons, Sean and Dean Kiner in Los Angeles. His website is *www.kevinkiner.com*.

Introduction

I assume that since you're reading this book you are interested in writing music for television. Perhaps you also have an interest in making money! Well, who doesn't? We all share common needs and desires: We enjoy eating; we appreciate having a roof over our heads, and; we despise the thought of wondering where our next paycheck will come from.

I also assume you enjoy writing music. In fact, I bet it's a passion for you! As creative artists, we pursue our craft for no other reason than that it gives us great joy. And wouldn't that joy be even greater if we got paid for what we love to do?

I'm here to tell you it's possible to not only write music you love to write, but to write beautiful music that is played on television. Your music played on television shows you yourself watch...on television shows you *don't* watch...even on television shows you've never heard of!

Music that appears in television shows is there for a reason. Music shapes the emotional context of a scene. It has *impact*. It defines *how* we're supposed to feel when watching the action on the screen. The right music fits. The wrong music will stand out like a sore thumb and distract us from what we're watching. As composers, we have great power to manipulate the audience's emotional psyche. And with great power comes - you guessed it - great responsibility!

At this point you may ask yourself some questions: How do I know what the proper thing to write is? Is this a skill that can be learned or do I have to be "born with it"? Once I have written music, how do I get it placed in a TV show? After my music gets used in a show, who pays me? Will I get paid every time that show airs? Should I put down a deposit on a yacht right away? Will the paparazzi leave me alone now that I've entered celebrity-ville?

Whoa! Hold your horses, partner. Slow down. Take a breath. Let's take this one step at a time. While it's true that successful composers can make a comfortable living writing music for TV, plan on it taking time. You're building a business. You're an entrepreneur now. Sure, you'll be your own boss and work you own hours, but be prepared to work hard at it. You'll only get out of it what you put into it.

The goal of this book is to point you in the right direction and arm you with enough ammunition you can trim years off of the learning phase and save a few gray hairs in the process (it may be too late for me, but save yourself!). The music business can be cut-throat and you may find it difficult to find the right information as you navigate through the rough waters of composing for TV.

As you'll learn, there is more to just writing music - *no matter how great it is* - to succeed in this business. The more educated you are in *all aspects* of the business the more likely it is that you'll flourish and be successful. As an old friend, Bob Vincent, once told me, show business is two words: Show and Business. You can't have one without the other.

I know, you want to focus on writing music, right? But that's where most people fail. Unless you can afford to hire a team of experts (managers, agents, publicists, attorneys, orchestrators, engineers, assistants, etc.) then you will do it yourself. While, for example, you can't be expected to have the same knowledge as an attorney who spent years in law school, you *can* educate yourself enough to make informed decisions regarding your career and business. And the more you know the easier it will become.

THE INTERVIEWS

I had the privilege of interviewing some folks who are not only extremely talented and highly successful in the industry, but are also really great people. I asked their opinions based on their own experiences working in their respective fields. You will find these quotes sprinkled throughout the book as *"words of wisdom"*. These featured quotes come from composers Matt Hirt, Tracey & Vance Marino, and Lydia Ashton, music library specialists Jeff Rona (Liquid Cinema) and Edwina Travis-Chin (APM Music), music supervisor Jen Malone, and music attorney Erin M. Jacobson.

LET'S GET STARTED

To begin with, let's get acquainted with the rest of the business that pertains to writing music for TV. It will pay off in a big way when you have a good foundation to work from.

PLEASE NOTE: This book will focus on *instrumental music*, not songs with lyrics. The placement of songs in television is treated differently due to that fact that words being sung compete with dialogue. Songs therefore have fewer placement opportunities. That being said, if you are a songwriter you will still find useful information here. Everything regarding the business aspects of writing music for television will apply to both instrumental and lyrical songs.

The following is a list of the chapters in this book and a brief description of what is covered:

PART 1 - DEFINING PRODUCTION MUSIC AND ITS USES

CHAPTER 1 - A Short History of Music in Film & TV

Music in film has evolved over the last 100 years: From a lonely theatre organist to full symphony orchestras. Television came along and changed the landscape with smaller budgets and smaller orchestras. Learn how TV shows use music today and what has changed over the past 20 years.

CHAPTER 2 - The Production Music Market: Who Needs Your Music?

Production, or "stock" music permeates the television landscape. Learn about how music libraries are "brokers" for your music and how they will get your music on TV.

INTRODUCTION

CHAPTER 3 - Music Libraries
Find out the nitty gritty of working with music libraries, where to find them, how to submit music to them, and how to build lasting relationships with them.

CHAPTER 4 - Musical Genres Used on TV
Learn the difference between musical genres and musical styles, what are the most asked-for genres, and who uses what specific genres and styles.

PART 2 - COMPOSING MUSIC FOR TV

CHAPTER 5 - What is a Cue?
A cue is the piece of music you are creating to be used in a television scene. This chapter will define the structure of the cue and will discuss the elements that make this the proper cue for a scene.

CHAPTER 6 - Writing Production Music Differs from Writing to Picture
Learn about how writing production music is both similar and different than if you were scoring music for a film. The focus here is on how to make your cues successful.

CHAPTER 7 - Write to Your Strength
Can you write music in many different styles? Should you? Learn how it's important to focus on what you do best.

CHAPTER 8 - The Composing Process
This chapter discusses the various techniques for actually sitting down and writing music. Learn how to be efficient and develop the discipline to do this consistently, day-in and day-out.

CHAPTER 9 - Finding Your Muse - How to Stay Focused

What is writer's block? Do you suffer from it and how can you avoid it? Learn some useful techniques for overcoming this debilitating condition.

CHAPTER 10 - Collaboration

Do you write alone or with other composers? Find out how collaboration can be beneficial to your productivity and can improve your overall composing skills.

CHAPTER 11 - Quality vs Quantity

Is it better to write lots of material at the risk of inferior quality? Find out if this is the best option for generating more income.

CHAPTER 12 - Managing Your Time

If writing music is a part-time career at the moment, learn effective ways to manage your time and still be productive.

PART 3 - TECHNICAL ASPECTS

CHAPTER 13 - Recording Your Music

Whether you are working strictly "in the box" with MIDI or recording live instruments with microphones in an actual recording studio, you will learn some tips on improving your workflow.

CHAPTER 14 - Using Sample Libraries

Sample libraries have become affordable and indispensable in creating production music. Learn about what the best libraries are for your particular needs and learn how to stand out from the rest of the crowd when using them.

INTRODUCTION

CHAPTER 15 - Mixing and Mastering
Find out if you need to hire an outside team to mix and master your recordings. Learn how to make your tracks "broadcast quality".

CHAPTER 16 - Stems and Other Deliverables
Learn about what is expected when delivering your music to the client. Learn what stems are and when you need to provide them as well as other assets.

CHAPTER 17 - Backing Up Your Tracks
You only need to lose your data once before you realize you need a backup strategy. Learn about the various solutions for backing up your data on a regular basis.

CHAPTER 18 - Organizing Your Life
Learn the importance of proper organization techniques. Find out if you need special management software to track what will eventually become thousands of tracks over years to come.

PART 4 - MONEY MATTERS

CHAPTER 19 - How Much Money Can You Make?
We all want to make money for what we do. Find out where the money comes from and how you can maximize your return on investment.

CHAPTER 20 - Performance Rights Organizations (PRO)
If you want to make money you will need to belong to a performance rights organization (PRO). These are the entities that collect money on your behalf. Learn how royalties are calculated and when you get paid.

CHAPTER 21 - Contracts and Other Legal Stuff

Legal concerns are often ignored by composers. Learn why it's important to understand even the most basic concepts of contracts to protect yourself - and your livelihood - from financial ruin.

CHAPTER 22 - Your Music as a Business

Learn the importance of treating your composing work as a business. Whether you're a sole proprietorship or a corporation, you will want to understand the ins and outs of how to run a business.

PART 5 - NETWORKING AND SOCIAL MEDIA

CHAPTER 23 - Promoting Your Music Through Social Media

You don't work in a bubble. Find out how to promote your music with the various social media outlets. Understand where to put your time and energy to build your business.

CHAPTER 24 - Networking

Like any other business, the music business is built around relationships. Learn how to network with those who will influence and impact your career. Find out where to meet the right people and what to say to them when you meet them!

CHAPTER 25 - Finding Other Outlets for Your Music

You've placed your music on television, so what's next? Learn about additional ways to get your music placed outside of the TV world to increase your income stream.

PART 6 - EPILOGUE

CHAPTER 26 - Where Do I Go From Here?

Is it possible to know everything there is to know about the music business? Not likely. Learn about things you can do to keep you in the loop for when the next big thing comes around so you can be ready!

WRITING PRODUCTION MUSIC FOR TV

Part 1

Defining Production Music and Its Uses

Chapter 1 _____

A SHORT HISTORY OF MUSIC IN FILM & TV

"A film is – or should be – more like music than like fiction. It should be a progression of moods and feelings. The theme, what's behind the emotion, the meaning, all that comes later." - **Stanley Kubrick**

Music as an Emotional Tool

If you ever get the opportunity to watch a scene from a movie before the music track is added, do it. It's one of the most eye-opening experiences you can have as a composer. When most people (civilians, not composers) watch a movie, they are often unaware that there is music being played in the background. Just ask them, "What did you think of the music score?" and you might get the answer, "There was music?".

But not us. As composers, we are constantly aware of music's presence, because of our interest in writing music for film we analyze how the music is working in the scene. But what does it mean in those moments when we *don't* hear the music? Does it mean we've failed as composers? As musicians? As artists?

No. It means that the composer did a superb job of writing music that was felt and not *heard*. Well, of course you heard it, but it was stuck in your subconscious. A film composer's job is to make you feel an emotion: fear, anger, sadness, joy. This is why it's so educational to experience viewing a movie scene before the music is added. Without the music, these emotions may not be apparent. A composer can manipulate your emotions in a way you may not even know of. This is the composer's super power.

Does this mean that music should never be heard? Should it always be at a subliminal level? Of course not! What would Indiana Jones (*Raiders of the Lost Ark, John Williams*) be without his march theme? Or Axel Foley (*Beverly Hills Cop, Harold Faltermeyer*) without his bouncy synth bass-driven theme? Both themes are examples of music scores that trigger an instant emotion and provide an unforgettable association with the main character.

Throughout the history of film, music's primary job has been to manipulate your emotions - to make you feel one way or another, even if the action on the screen appears otherwise. For example, in Steven Spielberg's *Jaws* (1975, Universal Pictures) we see families with children frolicking on the beach, not a care in the world. Without ever seeing the shark we only need to hear those two low and ominous notes (you know which ones) to know something foreboding is coming. John Williams' brilliant score has manipulated the audience to experience fear just by creating two notes - E and F, just a half step apart - to represent something horrific and primal.

Composers spend a lifetime learning and understanding different ways to trigger various emotions from their music. We learn early on that songs in major keys are happy, more uplifting, and songs in minor keys are sadder, more melancholy. These are generalizations, but you get the idea. Understanding how to manipulate emotions with music is the key to success to writing music for TV.

Film Music Before It Was For Film

Movies are stories with music. So is opera. Long before we could document these stories on film, operas were performed with an orchestra, live on stage before an audience. Movies and modern day musicals, have their roots in opera. Stage plays have existed for centuries, but operas - which are almost *entirely* sung - resemble modern day film to commingle music with the story to convey emotion.

Since the 17th century, opera dominated the entertainment world. Although opera still continues today as a form of musical theater, everything changed after cameras were invented and techniques for creating "moving pictures" began a new industry.

The first filmed stories were silent. No dialogue, no sound effects, and no music. Dialogue was remedied by inserting "cards", still images of lines of dialogue and other story points. But music and sound effects needed to find a different solution.

Theaters incorporated live musicians to accompany the film, often a solo pianist or organist. The larger the venue, the more money was available for larger ensembles. These keyboardists would perform music while watching the action on the screen. Along with the keyboardist you might find a drummer whose job it was supply various sound effects such as sirens, animal noises, sleigh bells, and horse clopping. Figure 1-1 shows the items a drummer would have used from an early 20th century Ludwig catalog:

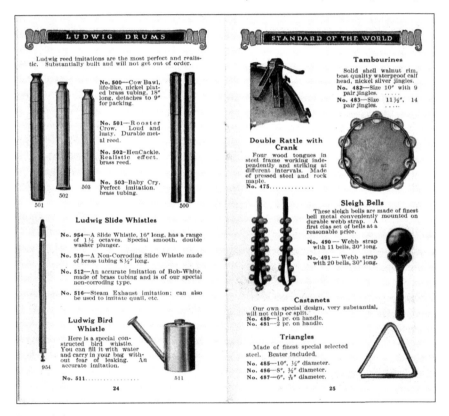

Figure 1-1

The music they performed was improvised or taken from a book of "cues" that were assembled to fit the need of any potential film. This was the first example of "stock" music cues. The repertoire that the musicians played comprised existing classical music or music from "photoplay" scores. These photoplay score books offered various pieces suitable for any imaginable scene: a chase scene, a fight scene, a love scene, etc.

In 1927, the first talking picture ("talkies"), *The Jazz Singer* starring Al Jolson was released. Introducing synchronized sound changed the young industry once again. Ironically, *The Jazz Singer* featured only about two minutes of synchronized talking. The rest of the dialogue relied on using silent picture cards. But the songs - music and vocals - were synchronized to the picture!

Early days of film production tackled the musical numbers - singing and dancing - by having the actors perform live to the orchestra off-camera while the actors sang and danced the songs on-camera. As technology improved, a separate music track could be added to the film after the fact, i.e. *post production*. This was the beginning of film scoring: writing music based on timings to match the action in the film.

Needle Drop and Other Forms of Stock Music

For a variety of reasons, primarily budget constraints, not every film could use the same size orchestra to score it. Films starring lesser known actors ("B" movies) demanded lower budgets which restricted the number of musicians that could play on the soundtrack. To solve this problem, clever solutions were needed.

If, for example, a film contained a scene that required a piece of classical music - perhaps being played on the radio - rather than having to write an arrangement of the piece to be recorded by the soundtrack orchestra, filmmakers would drop in a piece of pre-recorded music from a library of phonograph records. Hence the term "needle drop" as the needle literally dropped onto the record to play the music. Phonograph records were replaced with magnetic tape, but the name stuck.

Needle-drop, or "stock music" became a new industry. Music libraries, contained within the movie studio, provided the music cues to fulfill any musical need. As music departments grew within the studios, staff composers assigned to working on one picture would find their music cues re-purposed in other films as cost-saving devices.

Henry Mancini is an example of a staff composer at Universal Pictures in the early 1950's writing scores for horror films. Many of his cues were reused multiple times in other horror films of that era.

Henry Mancini

Stock music as a business model has grown over the years. While in the early days it was a way to handle issues that came up when it was unfeasible or unaffordable to record the music as part of the original score, today it has become an industry of its own.

The Role of Today's Composer

Mostly, music for feature films has remained constant: a custom music score is created only for a motion picture. But while a single composer is assigned the job of writing the score, it is not uncommon today to see a team of composers writing under the tutelage of the primary composer. The goal is for each member of the team to adhere to a predefined style of writing and orchestration. It should be as cohesive as possible.

In television scoring, much of the same can be said. It has been the tradition to use a single composer to write the scores for each episode of a series. But as deadlines have shortened, it has become necessary for teams of composers to work on a series. Often, multiple teams will alternate episodes to meet the demanding weekly schedule.

Scripted television shows such as *The Simpsons*, *CSI*, *Law & Order* (any of the many incarnations), *Family Guy*, *Game of Thrones*, and others, rely on a specific sound in the musical score. Any deviation in the musical soundscape would take the viewer out of the comfort zone that is "their show". But for reality TV, that's another story...

Reality Television

Reality TV, or "unscripted" television has been around since TV began. Game shows are by definition unscripted. The growth of cable TV has brought us hundreds, if not thousands, of channels. And every one of those channels needs content. The answer: Reality TV.

Most cable channels are working with a budget that is microscopic compared to that of network channels (ABC, CBS, FOX, NBC). And because the budgets are smaller, most shows airing on cable channels cannot afford to hire a composer to score every episode, especially if the show airs multiple times per week!

The solution then is to use library, or "stock" music. Most reality television shows feature wall-to-wall music. It is an unwritten rule that no silence is allowed. Drama doesn't unfold on reality TV the same way as it does for scripted shows. If there is a lull in the conversation there must be sound happening, and that sound is music. If you hear silence, it's rarely more than a couple of seconds.

This means that reality television requires LOTS and LOTS of music. This is where *you* come in. Since so much music is used, there needs to be an endless supply of music available to choose from. Unlike scripted shows where the sound of the music is consistent throughout, this is not possible with reality TV. There would not be enough music in a stock music library by a single composer that would satisfy the needs of the show without the music repeating itself too often.

Since music in reality TV is not being written by a composer for the action in a scene (scored) it is now the music editor's job to become the film composer. And by calling the editor a "composer", the editor now has the responsibility of choosing music cues that meet the emotional requirements of scenes that are being edited.

As a composer, you have the luxury of writing music that changes direction as necessary to enhance the visuals. If a character on the screen is crying, the music should reflect this in a supportive way. And if the character becomes happy, the music should address that in an equally responsible way.

> *"Library music is "applied music". It's never meant to be the starring player, it's there to support whatever else is going on."*
> *- Edwina Travis-Chin, APM Music*

Now imagine you're the music editor. When the person is crying, you must find the appropriate music that supports this emotion. And again, when the person's mood changes to happy, the editor must find appropriate music for *that* emotion.

This makes the job of the music editor very challenging. A composer could write the proper cues, but the editor is tasked with hunting down appropriate cues from within a massive catalog of cues. Watch a reality show and focus on how the music is incorporated into each scene. You will notice that the music will change often, from as little as every two seconds, or 15 seconds, or maybe 27 seconds. Rarely will you hear the same piece of music being played longer than 60 seconds. The music editor is attempting to emulate how a composer would approach the scene and apply the same emotional considerations as the scene unfolds.

The Future of Music in Television

It's a safe bet that the need for original music will continue to grow for the unseen future. It's unlikely that you'll ever hear a music production company say, *"Hey, we're good. We have enough music to last us the next 20 years!"* This will *never* happen. Music styles are evolving into something new and exciting, changing yearly, monthly, sometimes even daily. Television shows, advertising, video games, and every other medium that uses music will always want to reflect what's popular in contemporary culture.

Tools will continue to improve allowing composers to produce amazingly realistic sounds based on sounds of actual musical instruments. New and never imagined synthetic sounds will drive whole new genres of music. But whatever tools are available, nothing will replace the creative mind of the composer. Even as continued research into artificial intelligence and algorithmic composition tools are invented, it is unlikely any will replace the human mind.

Television as a medium will continue on. It's possible that movie theaters will disappear, just as drive-in movie screens have. Feature films will migrate to whatever viewing device is popular. We've already seen growing use of watching video on smartphones, tablets and computer screens.

As for composers, they will still need to possess empathy (cognitive, emotional, and compassionate) to create music that supports the story unfolding on the screen. The decision-making process to accomplish this requires analytical (left brain) and creative (right brain) analysis, i.e. actual intelligence, not artificial.

And those two brain hemispheres will make beautiful music together.

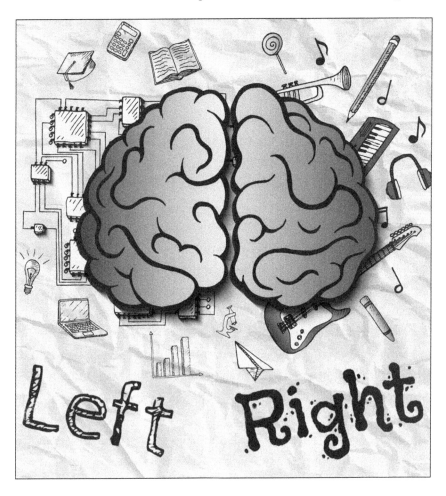

Chapter 2 _____

THE PRODUCTION MUSIC MARKET:
WHO NEEDS YOUR MUSIC?

"If opportunity doesn't knock, build a door." - **Milton Berle**

Music Libraries - The Keys to the Kingdom

Music libraries, also known as *Music Production* companies are by far the most common resource for composers for placing their music in television shows. A music library acts as a broker for your music. Music libraries are content providers: they find the shows that need music and supply that music to them.

The more music you have in a music library's catalog the better your chances that your tracks will find a home in a television show or film. But this is not guaranteed. There are several reasons for this:

- A library may supply music for an ongoing series, for example *Keeping Up with the Kardashians*. The show has aired for several seasons and could air for several more. The production team for the show requires fresh music and will request new music each season - if not more often. This is a good position to be in for the music library and your chances of placing your music in the show is above average.

- A library is pitching their services to a new television series, or an existing series is requesting new music. Your music *may or may not* be included in the pitch. The show may not even care to do business with the music library for a variety of reasons. Now your chances for placing music are below average.

- The music library is a new business - a startup. They are building their catalog from the ground up - OR - an existing library is revamping their current catalog looking for fresh new material to remain competitive. Either way, your music may "sit on the shelf" for an undetermined amount of time. It may get selected for use somewhere, but more often than not it will continue to sit and collect dust. Chances of success: well below average.

There are several strategies to consider, depending where you are in your career. In the beginning, it makes sense to get your music in as many music libraries as possible. This will improve your chances of getting a placement from *something*. This allows you to educate yourself which library is better suited to what you offer. If you are a Hip Hop composer you might discover that Library A has many connections in the market for this style of music, but Library B almost never places Hip Hop tracks.

> *"We look at the content being pitched to us to determine if it's different than what we already have. Is there something unique about it and so outstanding that we can't pass it up? Does it already duplicate something we already have in our catalog? If so, is it an area where we can't get enough of it, or where there's so much demand for it that we have to continually refresh the catalog?" - **Edwina Travis-Chin, APM Music**

Another strategy is to be involved in a library that requests music for specific projects as the need arises. For example, a travel show needs to use music that depicts a particular locale for that week's show. They could have gone to any music library and selected existing ethnic music from their catalog. In this hypothetical scenario, the show needs music that not only satisfies the requirements of cultural identification, they would like the music to be contemporary *and* feature a Hip Hop beat. Because this is a unique situation the music library may request new music from their existing roster of composers. Here, the chances of placing music on the show is well above average!

A very poor strategy is to "put all your eggs in one basket". Don't limit yourself to a single music library, no matter how successful they have been for you. If for any reason this music library ceases to be productive for you, then you are starting over. Find new libraries to represent your music while working your way up the ladder again.

Music libraries are analogous to the stock market. It would be a bad idea to invest all of your money (your music cues) into a single stock (music library). As the stock's value increases or falls, you risk losing everything. Any good financial broker will tell you to diversify. The same applies to your music. This is *your investment into your future!*

What Makes a Good Music Library?

There are thousands of music libraries all over the world. Like any business, they range from very poor (don't waste your time) to exceptional. What makes them good or bad can be summed up by several things:

● **How many tracks they place**

The more tracks they can place, the more money everybody can make. Keep in mind it's not "how many" they place. Each placement has an intrinsic value. Even though network TV pays much better than cable TV, music in a network TV show that airs only one time (for example, a live sporting event) may make less money overall than a cable TV show that airs hundreds of times over its lifetime.

● **Types and quality of shows they service**

They may place hundreds or thousands of tracks each year, but if they are only finding placements on websites as opposed to TV shows, then your return on investment will be lower. Placing music on network TV is more profitable than on cable TV, but there are more opportunities on cable TV. Put your energy into where you can make the most money.

● **How big their reach is in the marketplace**

Do they have contacts all over the world? Can they gain access to network shows or only cable television? Do they have relationships with music supervisors? The ones that have personal relationships with the movers and shakers stand a better chance of placing music.

● Type and length of contract

Are they exclusive or nonexclusive? Do they offer a reversion clause? Can you remove your tracks? There is nothing worse than getting stuck in an arrangement where your music is not getting featured and placed. In those cases, it's best to find a different home for your tracks.

● How communicative and accessible they are

Are you able to talk to or email anyone when you have questions or issues? Are they being honest with you regarding the promotion of your music? Communication is important. If you cannot communicate with them, it may be a sign they may be in way over their heads to manage their business.

Where to Find Music Libraries

So where can you find these music libraries?

● Your first option might be to do a web search for "Music Libraries", "Stock Music", or "Production Music". Other sources include music trade publications such as *The Hollywood Reporter, Variety, Music Connection, Film Music Network,* and *The Music Business Registry* to name a few.

● Check out MusicLibraryReport.com. Think of Yelp but for music libraries. This site not only lists almost every music library around, they also have an active forum discussing the pros and cons of each library. While it may be valuable to get an idea of which library is best for certain types of music, remember the nature of the Internet is to only write negative reviews when someone has had a bad experience. Use your own discretion when reading these reviews.

- Taxi A&R (taxi.com) is a service that lists music placement opportunities. Many of the listings will result in getting your track(s) signed with a music library. Other times it will get your music to a music supervisor working on a particular show or advertising campaign. They also feature on online forum (forums.taxi.com) that is helpful and informative in improving your skills writing production music.

- Ask your colleagues. Everybody has an opinion and it helps if that opinion comes from someone you trust and respect. Beware of opinions you find on the Internet. Sometimes people have an ulterior motive. Proceed with caution.

> *"By watching TV shows and seeing the names of libraries in the end credits. We emailed them, said we like the music they're doing for the show, asked if they are accepting submissions from new composers"*
> **- Tracey & Vance Marino, composers**

Direct Sources: Music Supervisors

If music libraries are the keys to the kingdom for composers, then the music supervisors are the actual kingdom. The job of music supervision comprises several duties:

- They act as the liaison between the creative and business ends of the production
- They choose which music cues get selected
- They decide which music libraries to work with
- They may work with composers
- They negotiate licensing fees on behalf of the production
- They manage the creation of cue sheets and submission to the appropriate PROs

Music supervisors can be in-house employees of the production or may be independent contractors. It's possible for a production to use several music supervisors in film, but television requires a sole supervisor.

> *"We have a lot of clients in the sports market so anything sports-related like rock, driving rock, heavy rock, dramatic...anything that helps tell that story."*
> **- Edwina Travis-Chin, APM Music**

Music supervisors wield considerable power in deciding what music gets used in a TV show. Music libraries will try to submit music for consideration knowing they are competing with other music libraries.

If you can build a relationship with a music supervisor, your chances of consistent music placements are good. Once you establish this relationship, the music supervisor will have the confidence you can deliver the music they are asking for. And if this music supervisor moves on to a different show you will be one of the first composers to be called to supply music for them.

> *"There has to be a level of trust between myself and the content providers."*
> **- Jen Malone, music supervisor**

Where do you find music supervisors? A good place to start is the GuildOfMusicSupervisors.com website. They take part in many industry conferences throughout the year and this may be a good way to meet them. Look at the end credits of any film or television show. There will be a credit for one or more supervisors that worked on the project. Know that music supervisors are rather elusive. They know composers want them to listen to their music tracks for possible inclusion on their projects. Tread lightly here and be respectful. You don't want to destroy a relationship before it ever begins.

If you connect with a music supervisor and they are interested in using your music, bear in mind that they may expect you to have dozens of tracks available. Remember, you are competing with music libraries that can provide *thousands* of tracks to them. There needs to be a compelling reason a music supervisor wants to work with you.

Direct Sources: Advertising Agencies

Advertising agencies are responsible for ad campaigns for a company's product or service. If the campaign is TV or radio commercials (as opposed to print ads), the agency is responsible for all of it, from initial concept, to story and script, to hiring the actors, to shooting the spot, and finding the right music.

Just as films and TV shows use a music supervisor, so do ad agencies. The duties of the music supervisor are the same as for TV and film. TV commercials use an equal number of songs (with lyrics) as they do instrumental music. The proper music for an ad campaign is crucial, even more so than for a film or TV production. Typically, only a single piece of music is used in a commercial, so selecting the right one is a monumental task.

Unlike a TV show, the music selected probably won't be used in subsequent spots, even for the same ad campaign. The music license payout can be in the thousands - if not tens of thousands - of dollars. Getting your music in a commercial can be a very lucrative deal.

Is it possible to get your music directly to the ad agency? Yes, but it's not easy. Ad agencies rarely take unsolicited material. Your best bet is through any of the methods mentioned above. Getting to know a music supervisor can be beneficial. If they are familiar with your work then they would suggest your music if they feel you're the right composer. The music supervisor has an immediate trust relationship with the ad agency. Their word is solid.

The next route, as with television shows, is through a music library. The libraries also have relationships with these music supervisors. But they will be pitching dozens or even hundreds of tracks for the spot. It's a numbers game for them. The more they can offer the better the chances of something from their catalog being selected.

The Bottom Line

Everything that has been discussed has a common theme: *relationships*. I'll say it again. *RELATIONSHIPS*. People are more likely to work on your behalf when they know you and trust you'll do a good job for them. Nobody wants to look bad so they will only work with those who can strengthen their image.

I encourage you to work on building relationships on a personal level. Your bottom line will depend on it.

Chapter 3 _____

MUSIC LIBRARIES

"Find libraries which cater to TV shows that use the genres you write. Be sure to consider what you can bring to the table that is unique from the pieces that the library is already representing." - **Lydia Ashton**

How to Submit Your Music

Now that you've found some music libraries, you'd like to submit your tracks to them. If you found a library through a web search instead of some other introduction (personal or professional) you'll want to look at the music library's website. Some have an open submission policy. Be sure to read any Terms & Conditions regarding the submission policy.

> *"Typically, we don't accept pre-existing music, we only use the demos to indicate what we think the composer would be good at before we send them a brief (which is a detailed description of what we are looking for on a specific project) and commission some number of tracks from them. Never send MP3s as attachments to an email. A link to SoundCloud or a similar easy to use interface is always best." - **Jeff Rona, Liquid Cinema**

Most libraries will provide a list of acceptance criteria. This will include items such as:

- **Length of cue**
  Cue requirements vary in length. You may be allowed to submit anywhere from 0:30 to 3:00. Typical requirements are in the 1:30 - 2:00 range.

- **Endings**
  Cues should end with a "button" ending. This means it does not fade out. The music ends with a definite conclusion. There are exceptions, but button endings are the norm. They will let you know if fade outs are acceptable.

● Versions

Alternate versions, or "stems" are standard. The stems may vary between music libraries. Stems are alternate mixes, such as removing the melody or a mix of drums & bass only. Occasionally you will need to provide versions designed to work in commercials, so edits of 15, 30, and 60 seconds can be expected.

● Keywords and Metadata

A document, e.g. a spreadsheet, for each cue is required. This is necessary so buyers can search the music library's database by keywords. This helps the buyer find the music that matches the emotion, genre, and style they are looking for. Other metadata may include key signature, tempo, composer name(s), description and keywords.

Some libraries require that each track go through an approval process. The track may be scrutinized for sound quality, mix, composition, performance, and saleability. Depending on the daily submissions a library receives, expect a turnaround time for approval anywhere from 24 hours to 6 weeks.

> *"Libraries will vet composers, but composers must also vet the libraries as well. Look at the credits for the library to see what kind of placements they have and if they're current placements."*
> **- Tracey & Vance Marino, composers**

Other libraries allow you to submit *anything* you want. While this is an attractive proposition for the composer if you don't understand the music production market then your track may sit unused forever.

Other than submitting your tracks via a company's automated submission page on their website, you may be invited by the library to email tracks to them. This has a much more personal touch and it shows that for whatever reason, you've been pre-screened and the company wants to know what tracks you have available that you can offer them.

You may be asked to post your tracks on the Internet on sites such as *SoundCloud*, *BandCamp*, and *SoundClick*. Keep in mind that these types of sites come and go. It was not too long ago that MySpace was the de facto site for showcasing your music.

> *"You want to find companies where people are really good at the business side of things. There are a lot of companies out there started by composers that don't quite understand the business side, other than one or two contacts that are asking for music from them. That can be problematic because they may not make the best deals." - **Matt Hirt, composer***

A WORD OF WARNING: If you are asked to send a link to your music on one of these streaming sites, make sure it remains there **FOR AT LEAST ONE YEAR.** You don't know how busy a library is and when you can expect them to listen to your tracks. Make sure it's available when they do. If it's not there you may never hear from them again!

Communication Etiquette

Okay, you've been introduced to a music library and you've submitted music to them. What now? You'll be eager to hear from them, sign those tracks, get them placed in TV shows, and earn performance royalties!

> *"Don't be a pest about it. Contacting someone every day saying "Did you listen? Did you listen? Did you listen?" is not going to be welcome."* - **Edwina Travis-Chin, APM Music**

What's the proper etiquette for communicating with libraries? First, consider yourself a professional even if you've made no money so far in your career. From here on out you must present yourself in a professional manner every step of the way. And being a professional you must handle every business communication with tact and respect. Otherwise, you will find a lot of lost opportunities.

Patience is key in this business. Music libraries are run by very busy people. You're not the only composer trying to get your music heard. If you've submitted music to them, wait at least a month before following up with them, then no more frequently than every two weeks after that. Every communication from you should be friendly, to-the-point, and not demanding in any way. Just let them know you are following up on your submission. It's okay to let them know you have more music available if they like the first batch (You do, don't you?).

Email is the preferred communication method. That way they can address your message at *their* convenience. If you call them on the phone, you may take them away from some other important task. Phone calls are fine once you've established a rapport with them. Following up every two weeks is recommended. Remember, be patient. If they don't get back to you after about two months, let it go. Some libraries won't respond with a rejection letter. That's a shame, but it's better they're the jerk and not you! This is a small and close-knit industry. You don't want to have a bad reputation even before you *have* a reputation.

Handling Rejection

Rejection is normal. Try not to panic. There are many reasons your music has been rejected. As mentioned above, music libraries will accept or reject music based on any of the following conditions:

- **Sound Quality**

This is referred to as "broadcast quality". It means what it sounds like: You music must sound as good as anything else that you'll hear on television. One of the biggest culprits for this is inferior sounding samples, i.e., it "sounds like MIDI". If your violins don't sound like violins but rather like an organ, then either your samples are not up to par with modern samples or you failed to program the sounds with controller (CC) data and articulations.

● Mix

If you're uncomfortable with mixing your music yourself, seek the help of a qualified sound engineer until you learn how to mix on your own. Bad mixes will stand out - and not in a good way! Typical problems include too much bass, too much reverb, unbalanced instruments (one instrument is *way* louder than anything else), and unwanted noise.

Remember that when mixing for television, TV's still use smaller speakers than audio sound systems, and your music will be mixed in the background well below the level of the dialogue. Try to preview your music in similar settings. Otherwise you'll find out that your low frequency instruments may disappear and things like high pitched percussion (e.g. xylophone) may overwhelm the mix.

● Composition

What is a good composition? There is no single answer because music is art and art is subjective. Music theory suggests common elements of a good composition include techniques such as melody, harmony, rhythm, repetition, modulation, and resolution. Writing music for television is not the place for Avant-garde experimentation - unless they have requested such music.

● Performance

Maybe you're just learning the violin. Congratulations! But now may not be the time to perform this instrument on your track. If you're not qualified to perform an instrument at a professional level on your own then it would be prudent to hire someone who has that skill. There are many quality sample libraries available where you can supplement a digital instrument for a real one when you're not able to perform it yourself.

If you have timing issues - can't play on the beat - then you should consider quantizing the performance. There are tools available to quantize both MIDI and audio data.

• Saleability

Understanding the marketplace will save you a lot of time and aggravation in this business. Not every style of music is being sought after. If you write polkas, you will find a limited market for those songs. The exception is when a library requests that specific style of music. When that happens, you'll be at the top of the list!

In the meantime, find out what genres and styles are being sought after and focus on submitting tracks that are needed.

> *"I do my very best to respond to those who reach out. I appreciate the effort, and I like to express my gratitude even if we don't end up working together. Unfortunately, given the volume of submissions and our schedules, I can't always." - **Jeff Rona, Liquid Cinema***

So if you've been rejected and the music library has not given you any sign why (it happens!), try to look objectively at your tracks and see if any of the above reasons may be in play here. Just because one music library has rejected a track it may well be accepted by another. Try to learn from every obstacle.

Exclusive vs Nonexclusive

Some music libraries will only work with you if you sign your tracks to them exclusively. Some may allow you to sign nonexclusively, while others may offer a combination of both.

What is the difference? Exclusive means that the music library is entitled to exclusive rights in representing your music and pitching it for placements. You won't be allowed to have those same tracks in any other music library, i.e., a competing library. There are some very good reasons for this which you will see in a minute. In contrast, nonexclusive means that your music may be represented by many music libraries besides theirs.

> *"I favor exclusive because those libraries tend to work with higher end productions, and thus lead to better paying placements."*
> **- Lydia Ashton, composer**

Why would a library choose one business model over the other? Does one model favor the library over the composer and vice-versa? On the surface, it seems like the exclusive model is a better deal for the library, not for you the composer. So why would they also allow nonexclusive? Let's examine some of the reasons.

Here are attributes that each type of arrangement offers:

Exclusive
- You give up copyright ownership to the music library
- Limited use of your music outside of the library (if at all)
- Your music is valued more ($$) if it is not available anywhere else (supply and demand)
- Some libraries will pay an upfront fee to sign your music to their catalog
- Term may be in perpetuity (forever) while some will allow you a reversion (remove it from their catalog) after x number of years.

Nonexclusive

- Retain ownership of copyright
- The ability to place tracks in multiple libraries
- The ability to license tracks directly to buyers

TV networks may refuse to work with any music that might be available from multiple sources. When networks make *blanket license* deals (see below) with various libraries, in theory they could make blanket deals with several libraries all containing the *same music!* Now they're paying for the same music multiple times.

> *"It's good to have a mix. Non-exclusive works in certain parts of the business well. It gives you the opportunity to try different things with the same track. On the other hand, exclusive is the only one that will get you into foreign distribution, which is very important. It's a big market out there."*
> **- Matt Hirt, composer**

Should you choose exclusive or nonexclusive? It depends on what your short term and long term goals are. Both have pluses and minuses so you can't say one is great and the other is worthless. With exclusive, you risk having your music tied up for the term of the contract with no guarantees that your music will ever get placed. Some of that concern can be offset if the library gives you an upfront payment for each track. This payment can vary from $100 to over $1,000 per track. This arrangement is not as common as it used to be.

Here's an example of why nonexclusive can be problematic. Let's say you have a track in several nonexclusive music libraries and four of them pitch your track for the same opportunity. Which library does the music supervisor choose from? Does this become a bidding war? If the music supervisor chooses Library B because they offered the lowest price then Library B is the winner! But guess what? You, the writer, are the loser.

Your track could have made more money if it had been pitched by only one library.

> *"Whoever pitched it to me first is who I have to go for. I don't have to, but I think that's the fairest thing to do." - **Jen Malone, music supervisor***

As stated, there are many pros and cons when deciding which type of deal to choose. If you have any doubt, start off with a nonexclusive deal and test the waters. Get to know the libraries. Remember, they're working *for you*. If they're not treating your music in your best interest, fire them!

> *"Non-exclusive licenses may cast a wider net for where your music is being pitched, but also might undercut its value by being pitched by too many sources. Also, many music supervisors don't want to deal with music subject to non-exclusive deals." - **Erin M. Jacobson, music attorney***

Retitling Tracks

Retitling is commonly associated with nonexclusive libraries as a way to market and license the same music under different names. This strategy allows them to register these newly titled tracks and collect performance royalties from them.

Exclusive libraries may also retitle your tracks, but that is a business strategy. Since they already own the copyright they can change the track's name to better suit their cataloging methods.

If you are placing your tracks in multiple nonexclusive libraries, it is expected that the tracks will be retitled as they are registered with your PRO.

Licensing Music

A license of any type is an agreement, i.e. permission, to allow your music to be used in some capacity, such as in a film or television program. In exchange for this permission the copyright owner of the music will be paid a fee for this license. Whether *you* are licensing the music to the buyer or a music library is licensing it on your behalf, a fee will be paid.

There are cases when a license may be granted for free. Reasons for this includes business strategies designed to improve relations between the parties and to maximize the return on investment. This return may be in the way of *backend royalties*, i.e. performance royalties after the music has aired on TV. The purpose of such deals is to entice the buyer to use the music catalog (yours or the music library's) with little or no risk.

License fees collected by a music library may or ***may not*** be split with the composer. This is a condition of the contract that must be considered. If your music is licensed but never used (such as with a blanket license), you will see no money down the road in performance royalties. For that reason, it is preferable to receive *something* up front. If your music is guaranteed to see placements then it's worth the risk of not sharing in any license fees since you will make money later on from performance royalties. **TIP:** Always try to get a share of the license fees.

This can be a sore spot for some composers. The music library will earn license fees whether your tracks are placed or not. It's a win/win for them but risky for you. Something to consider when choosing a library to represent your music.

Types of Licenses:

- **Synchronization License**
  If the intended use is for film or TV, this is called a "sync" license. This name derives from the fact that the music will be synchronized to the film. This is the license you will be **most involved with** while writing production music. The amount of money paid for this license is called *"sync fees"*.

- **Mechanical License**

If the use is for tangible media such as records and CDs, this license is referred to as a "mechanical" license.

- **Performance License**

This license is used when your music is performed live in concerts, clubs, conventions, etc.

- **Master Recording License**

For use of a recording of music *someone else* has made. The difference between the Master License and the Sync License is that the sync license allows the license holder to re-record the music, e.g., a cover song, while the master license uses the original recording. Typical uses of this type are for compilation CDs.

- **Print License**

This license is for printing lyrics and sheet music *someone else* has created, such as for song books and sheet music.

Types of Licensing Agreements:

- **Direct License**

In simplest terms, a direct license is as it sounds: the music is licensed from the copyright owner to the buyer. The price of the license is negotiated with the owner. This license is used by broadcasters (such as radio). Direct Licenses are not subject to PRO negotiations.

- **Source License**

Similar to a Direct License, a Source License is a direct license, but this agreement is between the buyer and a production company (or other music distributor) who has already negotiated and secured the performing rights for the music. As with Direct Licenses, Source Licenses are not subject to PRO negotiations.

● Blanket License

The blanket license is the primary license used by consumers of library music. A flat fee covers the use of *any* music in the catalog provided by the music library for a period of time - often renewable annually.

● Royalty Free

The term *"royalty free"* is often used in a derogatory manner and leads to a lot of confusion. Royalty Free is simply a licensing model. Music that is Royalty Free is *not* free to use. A fee is paid to license the music, but there are no restrictions how many times it may be used, hence, no royalties are to be paid per use. For example, music is licensed for use on a website. There are no restrictions how many views there can be of the web page containing the music.

● Needledrop License

This is known as a "pay-as-you-go" type of license. For example, a buyer may license a specific 30-second section of a track to be used in a commercial. They are licensing the use of *only* that 30-second portion - nothing else in the track may be used.

● Rights Managed License

A *Rights Managed* licensing agreement is the opposite of Royalty Free. A fee, or "royalty", is paid each time the music is used based on various predetermined conditions such as the number of times it will be used. Rights Managed specifies *how* fees are paid for music use. Both *Blanket License* and *Needledrop License* fall under the category of a Rights Managed type of agreement.

Public Domain Music

Music becomes public domain when the copyright expires. The current copyright term in the United States is "life of the composer plus 70 years". Once the copyright has expired, anyone can record arrangements of that music. Typical examples are Christmas songs such as *Jingle Bells* and *Silent Night*. But *Frosty the Snowman* and *Santa Claus Is Coming to Town* are NOT in the public domain yet!

Why do we care about public domain songs? Creating arrangements of public domain music can be a quick way for you to build your catalog. Getting versions of these songs placed in TV and film will still generate the same sync licenses as your original music.

You can still earn performance royalties as a writer from public domain music if you include original elements to the arrangement. The amount you can earn is a small percentage of what you would get if you wrote an original piece of music. Each PRO calculates this amount differently, though.

With the amount of public domain music available, especially classical music, this is a great way to increase your income stream.

"Before you submit your music to any library company, do some research. Go to several library websites and just start listening to what's there, and see if you can hear what that music all has in common."
- Jeff Rona, Liquid Cinema

Chapter 4 _____

MUSICAL GENRES USED ON TV

"Tension, Suspense, Hip-Hop, and Dramedy...if that's all you do, you'll make some money in this business" - **Tracey & Vance Marino**

Why Use Music in TV?

Movies and television include music for a very important reason: Emotion. Music does not differ from any character on the screen. Music is itself a character but played by sound rather than a human (or an animal for that matter).

Music drives the emotional direction of a scene. Properly used, music can command the audience to laugh, cry, or shiver with terror. Take, for example, *Psycho*, Alfred Hitchcock's masterpiece, and the famous shower scene, where Norman Bates (*Anthony Perkins*), dressed as his mother sneaks up on Marion (*Janet Leigh*) and murders her with a knife. You'll never forget composer Bernard Herrmann's shrieking violins mimicking the stabs of the knife. Terrifying, right? Now imagine that same scene scored with the theme music from *The 3 Stooges* (a variation of *3 Blind Mice*). Doesn't quite have the same effect, does it?

A parody of the film Psycho *might* use something similar to the *3 Stooges* theme song if it wanted to portray the scene as a ridiculous send-up of the horror genre. But that's not what Hitchcock intended. He wanted to scare the bejesus out of you and that's exactly what he did.

The importance of using the right music for a scene *cannot* be understated. When writing production music your job is to select genres appropriate to the shows or types of shows you are targeting. What are the right genres? Let's find out.

Genres and Styles

What is a genre? It is defined as *"a category of artistic composition, as in music or literature, characterized by similarities in form, style, or subject matter"*. If you're instructed to write music in the Country genre, you will need some additional information. There are many flavors of Country music. To understand what is being asked for, you need to know which style - or sub-genre - is being asked for.

For example, the Country genre contains the following styles (sub-genres):

- Alternative Country
- Americana
- Bluegrass
- Contemporary Bluegrass
- Contemporary Country
- Country Folk
- Country Gospel
- Country Pop
- Country Rap
- Cowpunk
- Honky Tonk
- Old-Time
- Outlaw Country
- Traditional Bluegrass
- Traditional Country
- Urban Cowboy

Each style is different. They all share common elements in instrumentation (guitar, bass, fiddle, banjo, mandolin, Dobro, pedal steel, etc.), but each style has its own unique attributes that categorize it that way. If you're not familiar with each style you may run into trouble. For example, if they ask for *Outlaw Country* and you give them *Urban Cowboy*, although it sounds like "country music" to you, it will fail on the authenticity check.

Think of it like this: Someone asks you for an apple. Sounds easy, right? So you give them a red apple. But guess what? What they wanted was a green apple. Be sure to ask the right questions. At the very least, don't give them a banana!

> *"The most asked for genre for me is probably orchestral (orchestral quirky, orchestral dramedy, orchestral fanfares, orchestral drama, etc.). I am also asked to do a lot of piano and strings. Those pieces are usually sad emotional pieces." - **Lydia Ashton, composer**

For a complete list of genres and styles, refer to Appendix A.

Moods

Besides genres and styles, moods play into how each style is used. A mood or a feeling is a way to tweak a human emotion. Moods such as happy, sad, nervous, anxious, and tense all define how the music should make us feel. Moods range from happy to sad and everything in between (neutral).

Genres and Moods are not mutually exclusive. Any genre (Country, Rock, Hip Hop, etc.) can be written to convey a happy mood, or a feeling of sadness. If you're writing music for a cop show or investigative drama, the terms "suspense" and "tension" will come up often. But what kind of tension? If the show is based in Ireland then the proper tension might be Celtic-based. Don't assume that everything tension-based will feature hybrid-orchestral instruments with a pulsing bass line. Ask the right questions.

Here are a couple of exercises for you:

- Take any piece of music you've written and write down the genre (from Appendix A). Next, write down the sub-genre (styles, also from Appendix A). Finally, look at the list of moods (from Appendix B) and write down *every* mood and feeling that describes your piece of music.

- Pick a TV show you'd like to write for. Watch and listen to the music it's using. Write down the same information: What is the genre? What is the style? Then pick a scene and write down a list of moods and feelings the music is conveying. What is the *emotion* they want you to feel in that scene?

Do this exercise several times with different cues you've written. Understand what it is you're trying to say through your music. Do the same thing with various TV shows. Understand the musical language the show is using.

> *"We do a lot of research and put a lot of thought into what we will be doing next. Sometimes we note trends, sometimes something we see or hear something that so inspires us that we will create an album to explore that."*
> *- **Jeff Rona, Liquid Cinema***

The goal here is to deliver the right music for whatever you are being asked for. You want to intuitively understand how to achieve this. Learning a genre and style is the easy part. Understanding how to write an *emotion* is the key to the kingdom.

For a complete list of moods, refer to Appendix B.

TV Shows and the Music They Use

To be successful in writing music for TV you need to clearly understand the music that is used for any show. Once you understand what type of music each show uses, you can target specific markets and narrow your focus.

> *"Early on I broke into the business by doing things that were outside of the mainstream. But it's good to have a niche early on in your career, not try to do the thing that everybody else is doing, and just see what works."*
> **- Matt Hirt, composer**

Let's take a look at some popular TV shows and discuss what kind of music they use. Most shows have a primary musical palette, or sound, that is consistent from show to show. This gives the show its identity. Exceptions occur at special moments, for example, an episode may take place in a western town and the music for that episode might use music typical in westerns (cowboy stories).

● Dateline

Dateline (NBC) takes on subjects of real life mysteries, usually murder. Part investigative cop show, part courtroom drama. The music is dramatic with a modern "film scoring" sound. The overall sound is hybrid-orchestral. To build suspense you will hear pulsating ostinatos and deep percussion accents. Storytelling elements include arpeggiated guitars and piano. Most of the music is in minor keys. Much of the instrumentation is very sparse. You won't be confused as to the type of show this is by the music they use. The same music would also fit in ghost hunting types of shows. Heavy on suspense, tension, and mystery.

Keys: Minor (90%)
Tempo Range: 60 - 100 BPM (beats-per-minute)

- **Keeping Up with the Kardashians**

This shows follows the exploits of the Kardashian clan (E!). They are young and rich so the music features modern styles such as Hip Hop and other EDM dance styles. Humorous moments are interjected throughout the show which feature Dramedy style (pizzicato strings, marimba, xylophone, woodwinds, and percussion). Keys vary between major and minor as the emotions switch. The goal with this music is to keep everything lively.

Keys: Major (50%), Minor (50%)
Tempo Range: 80 - 150 BPM

- **Duck Dynasty**

Duck Dynasty (A&E) takes place in rural locations around Louisiana. Musical styles are going to feature Country- and Blues-based sounds that include acoustic guitar, Dobro, fiddle, banjo, harmonica, bass, and electric slide guitar. Major keys are almost always used. Not a lot of serious drama for this family that makes duck calls, just down-home livin'.

Keys: Major (95%), Minor (5%)
Tempo Range: 94 - 134 BPM

- **The Little Couple**

The Little Couple (TLC) follows the lives of Bill Klein and Jen Arnold. The main sound of this show is Dramedy. It is kept light because the diminutive couple often struggle to live in a world of big people. There have been many dramatic scenes over the years as they have worked toward having children and the many medical issues little people are challenged with.

Keys: Major (70%), Minor (30%)
Tempo Range: 85 - 140 BPM

Auction Kings

Auction Kings (Discovery) is one of the more diverse shows of the bunch. Styles cover a broad range from rock to dramedy to Hip Hop to blues. The energy and pace of the show is vivacious as the show's principles work in the competitive world of antique auctions.

Keys: Major (99%)
Tempo Range: 100 - 140 BPM

It's interesting to look at the overall tempo ranges between each show. You'll notice that investigative shows like *Dateline* run in the slow range (60-100 BPM) and pop culture shows like *Keeping Up with the Kardashians* run in the mid- to fast-tempo range (80-150 BPM). This analysis should be done every 6 months on a variety of popular television shows to keep abreast with trends in music production.

> *"Good Hip-Hop that's not generic and not lame is something that we need a lot of. Tension is always good. Good comedy cues are hard to find."*
> **- Jen Malone, music supervisor**

The Shelf Life of a Music Cue

When I speak about "shelf life", I'm referring to how long a cue can make you money. There was a time not too long ago when Dub Step was a very popular style and could be found everywhere. Popular culture in music is often copied in television so shows feel relevant and "hip". But soon everyone is using Dub Step, and before you know it everyone is tired of it.

That's not to say contemporary music is a waste of time. Imagine if you had placed a Grunge-style cue on *Seinfeld* (NBC) in the early 1990's. Seinfeld has been airing on syndication ever since. You would still be making money from that cue. But if that same cue had landed on *The Ben Stiller Show* (MTV, 1992-1993), unfortunately that show only lasted a single season and has not been heard from since (sorry, Ben!).

When considering what styles to focus on, analyze shows like we did above. Do you recognize any styles that have been around longer than 6-12 months? Guitar-based music like rock and country last a long time. These instruments have been part of our culture for generations and we're used to their sound and feel comfortable when hearing them. The same goes for orchestral music. Orchestral instruments have been around now for hundreds of years so their sound is one that will likely be around for a couple hundred more.

Synthetic sounds - both digital and analog - burn out quicker. Synth designers are constantly looking for the next great sound. And while it's unique for a while, there is a quick burn off. This is not to say that you shouldn't use modern synth sounds - quite the opposite. You need to stay current if you want to be relevant. Just understand that those types of cues will stop making you money quicker than cues created using traditional instruments.

About every 20 years there is a resurgence of that "old sound". Call it nostalgia. This is your opportunity to repurpose tracks you made a long time ago but have stopped earning you money. This is why it's still okay to write contemporary sounding cues.

Songs vs Instrumental Cues

The focus of this book has been on instrumental cues. Why not songs with vocals? You will certainly hear songs throughout shows, especially those with young cast members - like almost any show on the CW. Why aren't songs used more often on shows? Because songs with vocals will conflict with dialogue.

Songs find placements in montages and closing scenes. Part of the reason for this is that the lyrics have a major impact. Instead of music in a minor key that sounds sad, songs can have lyrics that literally say, "I'm sad"! Songs are used judiciously and placement is critical. Unless the show is a musical (for example, *Glee*) you will not find many songs used in TV.

> *"It's important to keep in mind that certain styles of music license far more than others, and certain emotional approaches are also more in demand. Each library has their own set of criteria, so always know what they are looking for and then do your best to fulfill that as best you can. "*
> *- Jeff Rona, Liquid Cinema*

Part 2

Composing Music for TV

Chapter 5 _____

WHAT IS A CUE?

"Don't say you can do everything. Chances are you can't." - **Edwina Travis-Chin**

Originating in theatre, a cue is a visual or aural signal for an action to occur, either by an actor or stage hand, or for an actor to deliver a line.

A quick note about cues as it's related to this book. When referring to "cues" we are talking about instrumental music that is intended for media such as TV. Other forms of instrumental music that falls outside of this category would include genres and styles such as Jazz, New Age music, Meditation music, and Epic music (trailer-like orchestral music).

The Psychology of Cues

The terminology for a piece of music used in a film or television show is known as a "cue". Throughout this book and the rest of the industry, these compositions will be referred to as cues or "tracks". You may also hear "song" as a description, but that term is reserved for music with lyrics being sung.

Cues have a specific purpose: Support the visuals, help tell the story, and emphasize an emotion. In traditional film scoring, music is used only when it is needed and never more. The constant use of music without purpose is considered "wallpaper". After a certain point its value is diminished - we will not hear or feel the music. A film with the right score is often not heard, but felt. Even though we don't consciously acknowledge the music we understand that it is present by how it makes us feel.

Proper scoring techniques use compositional tools such as tension and release: Building moments of unrest, up and down, over and over - not unlike a roller coaster - until it resolves. That's the ultimate payoff.

Composition Structures

Music should tell a story. There needs to be a beginning, a middle, and an ending. It needs to have a purpose. It needs to take you somewhere. How do you achieve this? By understanding common musical structures, or *form*. You may have heard someone say, "this piece is an A-B-A form", or "A-B-C-A form", or "A-A-B-A form", or something similar.

Even if you're not familiar with music theory and this terminology, chances are good that if you've been writing music for any length of time you already understand what these forms mean. If you are writing or playing or singing songs, you have heard of "verse", "chorus", and "bridge". A verse is a specific section of the song. Same thing for the chorus. And same thing for the bridge. A song that begins with a verse, followed by a chorus, then another verse is using the "A-B-A" form. Each letter (A, B, C, etc.) represents a *section* of the song. It's just shorthand.

For example:

Verse / Chorus / Verse = A - B - A

Verse / Chorus / Verse / Chorus / Bridge / Chorus / Chorus =
A - B - A - B - C - B - B

Intro / Verse / Verse / Chorus / Verse / Chorus = A - B - B - C - B - C

It doesn't matter what sections a song contains. "A" is not always the verse. It's simply a mnemonic to represent a section. Folk songs often contain a single section repeated over and over and over again. So even if the song contained 27 stanzas (verses), you would not represent it as "A - A - A - A - A - A - (etc.) - A", you would say "A - A - A". That's enough information to define its structure.

Music cues rarely use more than two distinct sections, i.e., A and B.

Why? A music cue needs to say just one thing. Too much variation will make it difficult for the music to be placed. Remember, the music editor it trying to use a cue to represent or emphasize an emotion. If the emotion in the music changes then it's likely that it won't follow what's happening on the screen because you're not writing to picture.

Why stick with one thing? Isn't that boring? Well, it can be. Music that is *too* repetitive won't get used. It needs to build. Remember, it needs to "tell a story". So how are we going to do that?

Telling a Story

Music needs to have a beginning, a middle, and an ending. I know I've said this before, but I want this to sink in. This is important. The music - *no matter the style* - needs to start with something small and build and build until it reaches the climax (the ending). This growth can be in tiny increments, but it needs to grow. I'm not talking about building the sound level from a whisper to an explosion, or ramping up the tempo from dirge-like slowness to faster-than-a-speeding-bullet. No, I'm talking about subtle changes in the composition, instrumentation, and orchestration so that the music can grow organically.

There are two ways we will accomplish this: *Form* and *orchestration*. Form is A-B-A. This is the predominant form used in production music. The reason for this is "theme and variation", or in layman's terms "do one thing, then do another thing very similar to the first thing, then do the first thing again (with some subtle changes)".

Sounds easy, right? It is. Let's walk through an example. To make this simple, we will write two pieces of music: An A section and a B section. Remember, we will be repeating the A section at the end (A-B-A). To keep it simple, limit yourself to writing something in the range 8 to 16 measures for each section. This will serve our purpose for demonstration.

If you're still not sure what an A-B-A form sounds like, let's use

Twinkle, Twinkle, Little Star as a template (figure 5-1). In *Twinkle, Twinkle,* each section is four bars long. I also chose *Twinkle, Twinkle,* because even if you don't read musical notation, I'm sure you know this song by heart so you should be able to follow along with ease.

Figure 5-1 / Audio Example #01

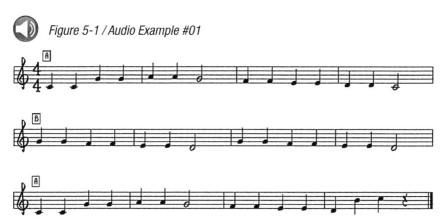

Each section of your piece will be at least 8 bars - twice the length of *Twinkle, Twinkle.* As in *Twinkle,* the B section will differ from the A section. But not so much that you think you are hearing a different piece of music. Our goal is to extend the language defined in section A. It's similar yet different. How? In *Twinkle, Twinkle,* Section B is the same as the second half of Section A. Notice it has a descending melody line? It never quite resolves, but that's okay because it's setting us up for returning to the main theme of Section A. At the end of the final A Section you notice that the last two notes differ from the original A section. I've taken the liberty here of changing the last two notes to help illustrate the point of the chapter. The reason for this is to add finality to the piece. It could have ended the same way as the original A section and that would be okay, too.

Twinkle, Twinkle, a simple children's nursery rhyme, is an excellent example of a composition that tells a story. It has a beginning (Section A), a middle (Section B), and an end (the final Section A). It has a definitive ending by taking the last two notes up an octave. Now how do we make this interesting? That's where arranging and orchestration comes in.

Earlier we talked about starting small and building to a climax. By keeping the instrumentation sparse in the beginning, you open the material up for expanding later on. It doesn't matter what style of music you're writing, whether it's rock, country, dance music, or whatever, the language of music is flexible and malleable.

As the piece progresses, introduce new elements - melodic, textural, or percussive - to keep the piece interesting. It must keep changing. If it contains the same instruments playing all the time, your ear will become numb. Keep the audience guessing! Drop out instruments from time to time to surprise the ear. Building up the complexity and suddenly dropping out everything but a single instrument can be startling and refreshing at the same time. Strive to make it interesting while moving the "story" along.

Using Melody

When we discuss "stems" in *Chapter 16 - Stems and Other Deliverables*, you will learn about creating versions of your cue. Common stems will include a version with the melody and one without. While melody is important, don't get too caught up in trying to be Mozart. If your melody is too busy or overwhelming, the editor will likely select a version of your cue that does *not* contain a melody. Or he may skip your cue entirely.

Why would this happen? Your melody must not conflict with the dialogue. It cannot be distracting from what's happening on screen. Melody is important. It defines the piece. The question becomes, how much is too much melody?

Figure 5-2 / Audio Example #02

Let's continue with *Twinkle, Twinkle* as our example. The quarter note melody throughout is non-stop. Since the melody comprises repeated notes, consider a version where we eliminate the repeated note and replace each quarter note with a half note (figure 5-2). The essence of the melody is still there, but we've opened it up and given it much more needed space. Now dialogue has a better chance of working with your beautiful melody.

> *"How can you protect yourself from unintentional plagiarism? You can't control the actions of others, but you can make sure your work is properly registered and keep track of everyone you send it to or that has access to it." -* **Erin M. Jacobson, music attorney**

TIP: Speaking of mixing melody with dialogue, here's a trick that's used with film scoring. When you're writing to picture you have the luxury of weaving melody in and out of the scene and around the places where dialogue occurs so it never interferes. In production music, you have no idea where the dialogue will be. So, here's what we can do: Write melody notes outside of the range of normal speaking voices. The vocal speech frequency of an adult male ranges from 85 to 180 Hertz, while the frequency of an adult female ranges from 165 to 255 Hertz. Obviously, these overlap. By eliminating the extremes (high for men, low for women), we are left with a musical range from 140 Hertz to 190 Hertz, around C to G (below middle C). This is not a wide range, but if we can increase our chances of getting our music used - including the melody! - then why not?

Titles

The name you give your cue should not be taken lightly. The title of your track is the first thing a music supervisor knows about your cue. For example, if your cue is titled anything along the lines of "Untitled" or "Final" or even "Final - Really Sure This Time", what does this tell the music supervisor? How on Earth would they ever know what type of cue this is? They could play it, but when they're dealing with hundreds or even thousands of tracks this is not a workable option.

> *"The title has to be interesting. This is your chance to describe your song in a way that would make the music supervisor click on it and listen to it. We like titles that are two or three words, but it has to make sense. If you have a song called 'Happy Song', no one's going to listen to that. But if you call it 'Sunshine in a Cup' you'll have a better chance of success."*
> **- Tracey & Vance Marino, composers**

But don't they rely on some kind of search tools to locate the tracks they need? True, but let's step into the music supervisor's shoes for a moment. Let's say they need a high-energy cue for a scene that chronicles competitive surfing in Hawaii. The music supervisor enters keywords into their library's search tool: "surfing, rock, hi-energy, sports action".

Let's say the search returned 500 results. This search will be for just one of over 100 different cues they need to find for the episode they're working on. They will not spend a whole lot of time previewing each cue and will stop as soon as they locate an acceptable one. Their attention will be focused on cues having titles that give them a sense of what kind of cue it is.

Give your cues a title that have meaning and will expedite the music supervisor's cue search. Be part of the solution - not the problem.

> *"Titles are extremely important. The title must be interesting sounding and descriptive of the piece of music. Users search for music using search terms. The first thing they look at is the titles. The title will stick out as intriguing or interesting and it also tells you what the track is going to sound like. It's just human nature to click on that first."* - **Matt Hirt, composer**

Intros

Since we know the music supervisor's job comprises selecting cues from hundreds of candidates, it's fair to say they will preview, at most, 5 seconds of your music. Within this short time, the music supervisor will know if this cue is the right one.

This brings up the topic of "intros" (introductions). How long should intros be? Should you have intros at all? Personally, I favor having no intros. I prefer to get right to it. But some cues demand an intro of some significance. This is a subjective, well, subject. My advice is, if you need to have an intro keep it as short as possible. We know music supervisors will not spend very much time previewing the cue to know whether its right or not. If they can't get to the meat of the composition quickly they'll give up too soon.

Button Endings

As we saw in *Twinkle, Twinkle*, my version of the piece ended with a definitive ending. It stopped with a single quarter note. Production music cues never fade out. How long of a note could we have used? A half note? A whole note? Even longer? Depending on the tempo it shouldn't linger over one or two seconds. Music editors will often use the ending of your cue to construct a version of your cue to fit a specific duration. This ending is known as the "stinger" (see *Chapter 16 - Stems and Other Deliverables*).

Edit Points

It is unlikely that your entire cue will be used as it was written. Music editors will only use small sections of your music to fit the scene they are working on. Typical uses range from 8 to 45 seconds of use. I have had cues run nearly two minutes, but that's more the exception than the rule.

Knowing your music will be chopped up, how can you ensure that your track won't be butchered into something unrecognizable? By building "*edit points*" into your piece. An edit point is a musically logical place where it makes sense to cut the cue. This does not mean you must insert moments of silence. If you do, that's okay, as long as the moment of silence make sense. Edit points are musical cadences or resolutions. Taking Twinkle, Twinkle as an example, the end of every fourth measure would be a natural point where an editor could make a cut.

Consider where edit points can go when writing your piece. The easier you make the editor's job, the more likely your cues will be used over and over.

Keep It Moving Forward

Your cue is telling a story. It's critical that you keep it moving. Like a shark, if your cue stops moving it will die. Give the editor a reason to use your cue for longer lengths of time. Let's say you have two bars in the cue that are amazing. In fact, so amazing that the editor loves to include those two bars whenever he can. Your goal is to have enough interesting material in the cue so that the editor does not abandon it after only those two amazing bars. You want him to use the entire cue!

Chapter 6 _____

WRITING PRODUCTION MUSIC DIFFERS FROM WRITING TO PICTURE

"One good thing about music, when it hits you, you feel no pain." - **Bob Marley**

Writing to Picture

In this book, we have been focusing on writing music for television from the standpoint of production music. But this is not the only way composers write music for TV. Like traditional film scoring, television composers are also engaged in "writing to picture".

Writing to picture involves having advanced knowledge of the action in each scene, and knowing what emotions need to be conveyed. This is accomplished by discussing the film (or show) with the director, reading the script (some do, some don't), and working from timing notes.

Also, referred to as "cue sheets", timing notes are critical for the film composer. The cue sheet is a list of events in the scene being scored. Events are notated by the timing where each event takes place. Timings are represented by the use of SMPTE time codes. Similar to a clock on the wall, timings include hours, minutes, seconds, and frames. This gives accurate locations down to 1/24th of a second (for film, 1/30th of a second for video).

The importance of the cue sheets cannot be understated. The timings listed on a cue sheet help the composer write music that synchronizes with the action on the screen to within a fraction of a second. If this sounds like complicated math is involved, you're right! Composers have had to rely on tools such as a click book. The click book is a large volume of timings that calculate beat positions for any possible tempo. Modern DAWs (digital audio workstations) feature a variety of tools to help with these calculations. In addition, two apps for Apple's iOS devices, *ClickBook* and *Film Scoring Tempo Finder,* are available through Apple's App Store, or HunkydorySoftware.com.

By having the luxury of knowing the timings in a scene, the composer can address every possible emotion with complete confidence. This is a desirable position to be in for a composer, because without timing information composers are writing blind.

Welcome to the world of production music!

Why Writing Production Music Is Different

If you want to write music for TV and you have not been hired to be the score composer you can still take part. Even television shows that are scored by a single composer (or team!) often supplement the score with production music. This can happen for a variety of reasons: Music outside of the show's style (such as music from exotic locales), the requested style it outside the comfort zone for the score composer, or source music (music coming from a source like a TV or radio).

The main distinction between being a score composer for TV and film and being a production music composer is that production music is *not* written to picture. Composing production music is based on hunches; logical deductions of what to write, the emotion to convey, for unknown events happening on the screen.

Basically, we're making educated guesses.

As you build your catalog with a variety of music cues, you must decide which genres, sub-genres (styles), and moods to write. There are two ways to accomplish this: Analyze the needs of the television industry in a thoughtful and meaningful way; or find a crystal ball.

What Production Music Is *Not*

We would love to create a musical cue that will fit in whatever scene a music editor is working on. There are many pitfalls with trying to do this. First, a score composer would look at a scene and write music that follows each action, each emotion, each setting that appears on the screen. Now imagine trying to accomplish this as a production music composer.

We can pretend to anticipate what will happen next, but this will only be a guess and we will most likely guess incorrectly.

"Do one thing. Do it well. Do it quickly" - **Jeff Rona, Liquid Cinema**

If you change the mood within your cue the way a score composer might do, any music supervisor or music library director would hear that cue and say, "I have no idea what to do with that!". The more your cue changes genre, style, or mood, the more likely it will be very difficult to place.

Write Cues the Industry Wants

Since crystal balls are hard to come by, we will resort to the old-fashioned way: Hard work, detailed study and analysis, and trial and error. Let's start with analysis.

In *Chapter 4 - Musical Genres Used On TV*, we looked at specific TV shows and analyzed the music used in each type of show. Let's take this a step further. As we did in Chapter 4, take any cue you've written, and...

- Identify the cue's genre
- Identify its sub-genre (style)
- List all moods that describe this cue.

Now, list all TV shows *currently on the air* you feel your music would fit in. Watch those shows. YouTube is a good source for locating episodes. Make sure you pick episodes within the last season or two at the most.

"We do a lot of work with television cable reality shows, music that supports those kinds of stories like light tension. There is a difference in my mind between tension and anticipation." - **Edwina Travis-Chin, APM Music**

By comparing the music that is used in those shows with your music, can you objectively say your music is a good fit? Turn down the audio in the show and play your music cue along with it. Does it fit the overall musical language of the show? Find a scene that evokes the emotion your cue does. Does it still fit? Does it feel organic?

Be objective. Step away from your ego for a moment. For you to be successful your music must not only be of the highest quality, it must meet the needs of the television industry. Are you a trendsetter? Music trends are often reflective of popular culture and the music created by radio artists. That's not to say you shouldn't try to set the world on fire with your new ideas. But this often comes from experienced and well-established composers.

The next method is trial-and-error. Once you've gotten your foot in the door of a particular show (your music is being used more and more and/or being requested by the music supervisor) you can stretch out [this is the *trial* part], musically speaking. You'll learn what works and what doesn't. If the music supervisor does not select your cue for placement then it's safe to say you've given them something they don't need or want [this is the *error* part].

After a while you'll intuitively know what they want. But don't throw that piece of music away just yet! Just because it doesn't fit for one show doesn't mean it won't fit for another. Chalk it up to the "learning curve".

> *"We frequently meet up with music supervisors and other post production people to show our new work, see what they're looking for in the future, and just make sure we can be as supportive and relevant as possible. We've produced quite a few albums that with a direct result of a music supervisor saying what it is they are looking for that is hard to find."*
> **- Jeff Rona, Liquid Cinema**

Chapter 7 _____

WRITE TO YOUR STRENGTH

"Without music, life would be a mistake." - **Friedrich Nietzsche**

Writing What You Know Best

The need for many styles of music can be overwhelming. As you watch the shows currently on the air you're noticing many different styles, but also a lot of the same styles. These shared styles are what's known as "musical trends". So, the question becomes, should you follow along with these musical trends and write what everyone else is doing or try to fill in the gaps with less common styles? In other words, follow the "road less traveled"?

This is a valid question and a very important one. It determines how we spend our time. Writing a lot of music that no one needs will be an exercise in futility. To figure out which direction to go, you need to ask yourself some tough questions:

- How many different styles of music am I comfortable writing?
- Of these styles, how many of those do I feel I'm an expert at?
- Have I ever written and produced music in those styles?
- Are any of these styles being used in television?

Consider the various styles of music you are comfortable with. Create a list of the top 10 styles you can write. Make #1 the style you are most comfortable with and you feel that this is your area of expertise, and #10 the least comfortable of the bunch.

If you don't have ten styles, then make a list consisting of however many you have, but not over ten. This list needs to comprise styles you have written or played (such as playing in bands). For example, it's possible to have great familiarity with Big Band music because you performed in those bands but maybe you've never written a piece on your own.

In the beginning of your career writing production music, it's important for you to experience success. That's why I want you to focus on styles of music you're comfortable with. Now, with your list of your ten best styles and starting with #1 and working your way to #10, which of those styles can be found in television regularly?

You will have at least one style that is being used on TV regularly. This is the style I want you to focus on the most for now. If you find more than one of your ten styles being used in TV, let's then reduce this list to only three styles. If none of those styles are being used, then we will talk about learning new styles in a minute.

The bar is high for quality music in television. Not only a high bar in terms of being polished (broadcast quality) and with good performances, but also in terms of authenticity. When you hear something created by someone who has no business doing that style of music, it stands out like a sore thumb! Don't be that composer.

Another reason for writing what you know best is output. You will produce many more tracks at a quicker pace when you are writing what you know and love. When you're learning something new, it will take that much longer. Your goal in the beginning is to build your catalog so you are marketable.

Learning New Styles

Do you want to want to stick with the styles you know best and no more? If you do, that's okay. Some people are happy writing a single style or two. If you're writing in a style that never goes, well, out-of-style, then good for you! Styles like classical, blues, and bluegrass almost never change. Those are safe styles. But there may not always be a need for them. That's why you want to consider learning new styles.

*"I spend some time researching and immersing myself in exceptional examples of that music style. I also read about that style. I pay special attention to scales, rhythm, and instrumentation looking for the DNA that sets that style apart from others." - **Lydia Ashton, composer**

Hopefully you're wanting to master styles you enjoy. Your love of a musical style will come across in the writing and performance. But if you are trying to produce music because that's what you think will get you more placements, you may find yourself dissatisfied and won't get the placements you are trying to get.

More than just being dissatisfied, a lack of authenticity will prevent you from succeeding. You must have even a moderate amount of interest in this new style. Treat learning a new style like going back to school. As we did in *Chapter 4 - Musical Genres Used On TV*, analyzing shows and the music they use, do the musical analysis to understand the components and structure of this new style. You will discover many subtleties that only come with detailed research.

Write in this new style. Compare your music in this style with those that are authentic and do it well. Be objective when you do this. Does it stand up to theirs? Use theirs as a model and keep working to match the energy, sound, and performance. When you feel you're ready, submit your tracks when the opportunities arise. You'll know soon enough when you can consider this new style mastered.

"Go to the libraries themselves and listen to the tracks they have in that style. We will listen to 20-50 cues to get a good idea of how the cues are formulated and structured, the instrumentation, and see if it works with the show. It takes a bit of research but it's worth it."
*- **Tracey & Vance Marino, composers***

Finding a Niche

You may find you are a niche writer. A style that few people are covering and you are the master at it. For example, you write French accordion "cafe music". There may not be as many opportunities for this style of music as, say, EDM (electronic dance music), but you'd be surprised how many times travel shows need this. If you can produce 50 or more tracks in this style you will find yourself in a good position to having active placements.

No matter what styles you know, make sure you work to your strength. This is the quickest way to make money writing music for TV.

> *"I do a ton of research. I immerse myself in the style I've never done before by listening to the top writers in the genres. My clients have high expectations of me so I have to do a lot of research so it sounds authentic."*
> *- **Matt Hirt, composer***

Chapter 8 _____

THE COMPOSING PROCESS

"Find out what the library needs first, then write that cue. Don't write a dated-sounding cue." - **Jen Malone**

The Blank Page: Getting Started

An artist will start with a blank canvas. A composer will start with a blank score...or to be more specific, an empty DAW project. Whatever the medium you're working with, the blank "page" is the scariest part of creating music.

Do you have a plan? Sometimes we don't. Sometimes we like to noodle around on the keyboard (or guitar or whatever instrument you use to compose with) until something "magical" happens. But what happens when that magic doesn't materialize? Let's talk about some ways to avoid this scenario.

> *"I always write to a target - almost immediately. I already know what the style is going to be and the opportunity that I'm aiming at. Even if I'm noodling around on the keyboard and try out some new sounds, as soon as I get some kind of a seed I immediately ask myself, "where can I go with this, make a useful piece of music that somebody's going to want to do something with?". I never complete a song and ask "what can I do with this now?". My efforts are targeted very early on."- **Matt Hirt, composer***

Since we're writing production music for TV, let's assume you have a specific genre in mind. If you don't, you should. In earlier chapters, it's important to know what type of show you are targeting and the genre and style of music you want to write. At the least, knowing the genre is the **single most important decision you'll make** when deciding to write a cue.

Great! Now we know the genre and style we're writing; the rest is easy! The next important decision is defining the **mood** you are creating.

Start with broad categories and narrow it down. For example, let's start with something that's sad. I don't care what the genre is you've chosen (rock, blues, country, solo piano, etc.), this mood can fit in any of them.

What kind of sadness is this? Depressed? Defeated? Down but optimistic? Be specific. What you choose defines your cue. Now, based on these parameters (genre, style, mood) it's time to give it a title. Why? This is how you'll stay focused. A cue's title is a way to define the scene you are writing. We can't know what type of scene this music will be used for, but by giving it a title you are "virtually" writing-to-picture. Picture a scene in your head. Make it specific. Write to that scene. Give it all the emotion you would as if you were writing-to-picture. Keep referring to this title to keep you writing what you intended to write.

If you name you came up with for the cue is "Death of My Father", you would have some specific visuals in your head that will influence your writing. If it was called "Failed My Driving Test", that sadness would be very different. This makes the sadness distinction much more specific than saying "this cue will be sad" vs. "this cue will be *really* sad". See the difference?

> "I usually sit down at my piano (midi controller) and start improvising. I usually record the improvising and go back later to listen through and save ideas that I like. It can be the melody, chord progressions, rhythmic ideas, or a combination of all three. Once I have a melodic idea and chord progression I decide on the format of the song (ABA etc.). Once I am ready to start recording I usually start with a bass line to lay the foundation everything is resting on, then add the melody, and then fill in the rest."
> - **Lydia Ashton, composer**

Working from Templates

Creating pre-built templates in your DAW can be one of the biggest time-saving devices you can use. A template contains tracks for each instrument you would use for writing a cue in a specific style. It would also pre-load any software synths needed. The goal is to open a template and start composing immediately. The easiest way to lose focus is to be interrupted by looking for the right sound and all of the mechanics required for adding tracks, assigning MIDI channels, etc.

Your templates are ever-evolving. As you find new sounds you like you are likely to keep tweaking your template until it is perfect. But it will never be perfect because even *newer* sounds will come into your life and you'll go back and tweak the template once again! Regardless, a template will save you tons of time.

Each template you create will contain common elements. The main difference between one template and another are the specific instruments involved in the cue you are writing. For example, if your cue is orchestral you will want to have all of the orchestra's instruments laid out. You will have sections for woodwinds, brass, percussion, strings, piano, harp, and choir. But if your cue is for a trailer, this will be a hybrid-orchestral cue. You can start with the orchestral template and add tracks featuring the hybrid elements: synths, drums, guitars, etc. And just like that - voila! - you have a new template.

Besides instrument tracks, you will want to include tracks for mixing stems. A template will also include various mixing buses, reverbs, compressors, equalizers, and other sound processing plug-ins.

Now you're ready to pick a track and record an instrument part.

Musical Templates

A musical template is using someone else's music as a starting point. I'm not suggesting that you use someone else's music and plagiarize them. We want to look at their music as a starting point - for structure, style, instrumentation, and arrangement. This is a useful technique when you are first learning a new style. Never plagiarize another composer.

As popular culture drives the music industry, it's common that everybody wants to feature what is hot. When the film *Birdman* came out (*2014, Fox Searchlight*), the film's composer, Antonio Sanchez, wrote a score featuring only drums. Because this was such a unique score, inevitably, music libraries would be interested in finding cues that were drums-only. Finding soundalike cues is a common occurrence. Much of the music library industry is based on finding music that sounds like something else. The danger is doing it in a way that infringes on someone else's intellectual property.

A case in point is the *Blurred Lines* lawsuit in which Robin Thicke and Pharrell were sued for plagiarizing music by Marvin Gaye (*Got to Give It Up, 1977*). The melody and lyrics were different between the two songs; however, it was ruled that the underlying music, the "groove", was copied. While it is not possible to copyright chord progressions, the judge felt that the intent was to copy the feel of the music verbatim. Whether this was the right or wrong decision, this was the result. We must tread lightly as production music composers when emulating someone else's music.

Now getting back to using others' music as a template...starting with a chord progression from another song, write your own melody to it. If this lights a creative fire under you, all the better. Again, don't rip off anything specific in the template's design. Just consider it a model for creating something new.

Melody or Harmony?

I'm sure you've heard this age-old question: Which came first, the chicken or the egg? This question can also apply to writing music. Do you begin with a melody or a chord progression? That all depends on you and what your strengths are.

If you use the method above and start with someone else's music as a template, you are starting with a chord progression. Now you need to add your own melody to it. At that point, you are free to tweak the harmony as your melody takes twists and turns not supported by the original chords. This a good thing. This means you are writing your own music.

Once you are coming up with your own chord progressions, the process is the same: Add melody that works with the chords.

Some people prefer to start with melodies. The hard thing about this method is that you have to then come up with a harmony that fits the melody you've written. It's common that the melody you're writing is being created with a harmony already in mind, but it's deep in your subconscious and you don't realize it yet.

Another popular approach - and this fits the noodling technique - is combining the methods of creating *both* the melody and harmony at the same time. For example, if you play piano you might start by playing a C chord with the left hand and finding a few notes that fit that chord. Let's say you're writing *Twinkle, Twinkle, Little Star* (our favorite example!). You play a C chord and play four notes: C - C - G - G

 Figure 8-1 / Audio Example #03

Your next notes are A - A - G. Your ear tells you that the C chord has served its purpose and it's time to change chords. You look at the various logical solutions for the note 'A'. You try F, Am, Dm (all diatonic chords in the key of C). Finally, you settle on 'F'.

 Figure 8-2 / Audio Example #04

Good choice! But the G melody doesn't sound right on the F chord, so it's time to search again for something else. I will spoil the ending here and let you know the best chord choice is C again.

 Figure 8-3 / Audio Example #05

You get the idea. It's a process and there is no one right answer.

Popular Chord Progressions

There are such things as popular, or common, chord progressions. These are chord progressions that occur time and time again. Take for example the 12-bar blues. This is an age-old chord progression that fundamentally never changes. In its simplest design, it follows this pattern (figure 8-4):

 Figure 8-4 / Audio Example #06

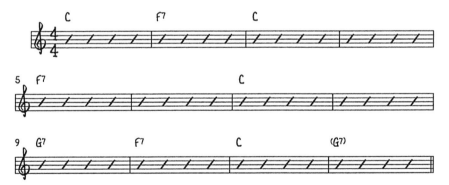

Popular chord progressions evolve. Songs in the 1950's (the doo-wop era) often favored the **I - vi - IV - V** pattern:

 Figure 8-5 / Audio Example #07

Regardless of the key, the pattern is the same. Today's popular songs frequently use the **I - V - vi - IV** pattern:

 Figure 8-6 / Audio Example #08

Songs that have used this pattern include:

- Let It Be - The Beatles (1970)
- Don't Stop Believing - Journey (1981)
- She Will Be Loved - Maroon 5 (2002)
- Edge of Glory - Lady Gaga (2011)

A variation of this pattern changes the order as **vi - IV - I - V**:

 Figure 8-7 / Audio Example #09

You may have noticed that in the last three patterns, they all use the same chords (C / F / G / Am) but in varying order. It doesn't matter what key you are in, the chords are related by their position in the scale. So, if you are writing in the key of G, the chords would include G / C / D / Em. Songs in the key of D would include D / G / A / Bm. The relationships between each chord is the same, regardless of the key.

Since these are such well-tested chord progressions, it makes sense to take advantage of their history and use them. If nothing else, they make a good starting point. Then make changes to suit your melody.

Relationships between one chord and another often imply certain emotions. University of Kansas music professor Scott Murphy has analyzed various relationships between one chord and another and identified their emotional connotation as used in film scoring.

Major keys:
- C - D : Protagonism
- C - F# : Outer Space
- C - Ab : Fantastical
- C - Em : Sadness, loss
- C - Fm : Romantic, also Middle Eastern

Minor keys:
- Cm - F : Wonder, transcendence
- Cm - D : Mystery or dark comedy
- Cm - B : Dramatic
- Cm - F#m : Antagonism, danger (less character-based)
- Cm - Abm : Antagonism, evil (more character-based)

Keeping It Simple

Writing production music often demands a simpler approach to composition. Don't over think what you're writing. If you were composing for the concert stage you might well compose very sophisticated melodies and chord progressions. But for production music, this is rarely the case. Often, the simpler the music, the more useful it becomes.

> *"Is this chord working? Is this note working? Is this sound working? Is this part working? Can this melody be better? Those decisions initially are what you spend a lot of time with and that's why you're slow. After a while you immediately know what's not working and know what is working. Efficiency comes from practice." - **Matt Hirt, composer**￼*

This also brings up the use of counterpoint. Counterpoint, or counter-melody, is a device that goes back to the days of Baroque music. The essence of counterpoint is creating alternate melodies that work alongside the original melody. Think of it as two people having a conversation where words often overlap each other's. It can be treated as question and answer, statement and response, or any other combination.

Use of counter-melody should be handled carefully. Remember, we're already dealing with fighting dialogue on screen with just our single melody. Counter-melody only complicates things even more.

Chapter 9 _____

FINDING YOUR MUSE - HOW TO STAY FOCUSED

"Writing music is a lot of problem solving" - **Matt Hirt**

Writer's Block

You sit down to compose music and stare at a blank page. The "blank page" is a metaphor for whatever medium you use to compose music. In *Chapter 8 – The Composing Process*, the blank page can be a blank canvas (for the artist), a blank score pad (for the traditional composer), or an empty DAW project (the modern composer). Whatever you want to call it, the blank page is what we all start with.

> *"Writer's block often comes when I am concerned that my music won't be perfect. Its root is in the fear that what I create won't be good enough."*
> *- Lydia Ashton, composer*

Do we always have a reason to write music? Not always. Maybe we have a project we're working on and have a deadline to meet. Other times we may write music for the joy of being creative. Either way, writer's block is a real thing and we all experience it at some point.

How is it that prolific composers like Haydn, Mozart, Bach, and Beethoven could create so much music over their lifetime? Even film composers like Max Steiner, Ennio Morricone, and John Williams have scored music for hundreds of films, often writing two hours' worth of music for each film.

There's nothing like having a deadline to light a fire enough for you to get the job done. But even with deadlines, even the best composers experience writer's block. So, if you are experiencing writer's block, don't feel like this is the end. There are ways around it; things you can do to overcome this temporary obstacle.

Throughout the book, I've emphasized "*emotion*" as a key component to writing music. Without understanding the emotion you're trying to convey, you will experience much more difficulty than you need to. Having a clear direction will eliminate a lot of the stress you might be experiencing. I believe the main reason for writer's block is not having a clear understanding of what you are trying to accomplish.

Chapter 8 also disseminated how chord progressions and the relationships between various chords imply certain emotions. Understanding which chord to use next to achieve the emotion you are looking for will keep the ideas flowing.

The biggest block is where to begin. This is half the battle! Not knowing what note to write first can prohibit you from getting anything done. Let's avoid that by writing something. Write *anything!* As an example, let's say you are writing something uplifting and forward-moving because you've already decided which genre, style, and mood to write. Evaluating between major and minor keys, we will choose a major key. A minor key implies something more melancholy and that's not we're looking for because we've decided without question what emotion we're going for.

For the sake of getting started, let's choose the key of C and pick a C major chord as the first chord. Next, looking at the list of chord relationships from Chapter 8, let's pick the first one, the protagonist theme. This means we'll start with a C major chord and move to a D major chord.

 Figure 9-1 / Audio Example #10

Let's add melody notes. Let's throw in the first four notes of *Twinkle, Twinkle, Little Star* to get us going. But we don't want it to sound like

Twinkle, Twinkle, so let's change it by removing the second note. Great!

 Figure 9-2 / Audio Example #11

Next, let's fill in some notes to fit the D chord.

 Figure 9-3 / Audio Example #12

So far so good. Let's repeat those two bars, but let's change the ending notes to make it resolve somewhat.

 Figure 9-4 / Audio Example #13

That was painless, wasn't it? Even if we later decide we don't like this theme we can go back and change it later. But at least we have *something!* I feel that doing *something* is always better than doing *nothing*. It gives you a feeling of accomplishment.

Coming Up With Ideas

I'm a firm believer of throwing nothing away. Especially if you're working against a deadline. There are always ways to improve something, but you must have *something* to improve upon it. So how do we keep these ideas coming?

> *"What's your musical vocabulary? I've developed a rich vocabulary over time which means I have solved many problems many times. When you've done that you rarely come to a problem that you can't solve."*
> **- Matt Hirt, composer**

One idea is rhythmic mimicry. Take any song you're familiar with. Of course, we will utilize *Twinkle, Twinkle* once again! Without regard to the actual melody notes, look at the rhythm the song uses for the first four bars:

 Figure 9-5 / Audio Example #14

Use this as inspiration for creating a melody. Since a composition consists of melody, harmony, and rhythm, working within constraints like this eliminates one of these components. Forcing you to do something you might not ordinarily come up with can be very motivating.

The next idea is melodic shapes. Look at a song and understand how the melody moves up and down. Does it take giant leaps (up or down a fifth or more) or use stepwise motion? Map out songs and use those shapes to mimic in your own music. In *Twinkle, Twinkle*, there is a moderate leap of a fifth at the beginning, but the rest of the melody uses stepwise motion.

Figure 9-6

We have already discussed the third option, harmonic mimicry. Starting with a chord progression from another piece of music is a good starting point for writing new music. You might start with the original chord progression but alter chords to fit your unique melody as you go. Try rearranging the order of chords to see if you come up with anything interesting.

Experiment with common tones. See if you can find a chord progression that works with a single note or a group of notes. For example, if you have a note C, chords that support that note are C, F, Am, Ab, F7, Cm, Eb6, C7, D7, Gsus, Fsus, etc. This is not even counting jazz chords!

Next, we'll look at analyzing music being used in television as a tool to writing music that has already passed the test of acceptable writing.

Deconstructing Cues: Listening and Analysis

One of the best ways to learn how to write the cues that are being used on TV regularly is to take the time to listen to those cues. Doing detailed analysis will help you understand the medium and of what works and what doesn't.

"Don't write a cue that sounds like every other reality cue that's ever been on television and sounds cheesy." - **Jen Malone, music supervisor**

So how do you listen to that music? Hearing a cue in isolation is challenging because often the music is buried behind dialogue and other sound effects. Listening to the music as it is played on a show is the first step. But a better way to hear those tracks is to go directly to the source: The music libraries.

Many music libraries have a public-facing page on their website that showcases the tracks in their catalog. Other libraries require you to be a client before being given access to this area of their site.

When listening to any cue, start with the analysis we did in *Chapter 4*

- *Musical Genres Used On TV*, by determining the genre, style, and moods it is evoking. Then, break down the cue by analyzing the following items:

- **Key**
Is it major or minor? What is the specific key?

- **Tempo**
What is the BPM (beats-per-minute)?

- **Length**
What is the total length? Does it fall in the typical range of 1:30 - 2:30?

- **Form (A - B - A, etc.)**
Can you identify the form? Is it typical?

- **Instrumentation used**
Identify every instrument used. Is this appropriate for this style of cue?

- **Identify any edit points**
Are there identifiable breaks that an editor could use?

- **Does it contain a melody?**
If this is a full version (not a stem), is the melody too busy or subtle?

- **What is the range of notes the melody covers?**
Is it suitable for working with dialogue? Is the melody appropriate for this type of cue?

- **What types of movement does the melody use (stepwise, leaps)?**
Does this type of movement work with dialogue or is it obtrusive?

- **Does it modulate or change keys?**

If it modulates, does it return to the original key? Is the key change necessary?

- **Do instruments drop out at any point?**

How interesting is the arrangement? Does it bore the listener by never changing?

- **When do instruments make an appearance?**

Does the cue build by adding instruments a little at a time or are they always present?

- **Does the cue use any hooks?**

Are there identifiable melodic or rhythmic hooks that make the cue interesting? Are the hooks overused or are they appropriate?

Using this data, compare this cue with one of your own that would fit in the same type of show and scene this cue was used on. Do you find any weaknesses with your own cue that can be improved by knowing this information?

If you're using this analysis to write a style new to you, try to follow what this composer has accomplished until you feel comfortable enough to vary the formulas used here. Consider it a learning tool, a mentor if you will. We're assuming that since this cue has been placed on a TV show, then the composer has done something right.

Chapter 10 _____

COLLABORATION

"Better to have the uncomfortable conversation up front rather than later"
- **Paula McMath**

Why Collaborate?

Composing music is often thought of as a solo endeavor. But songwriting duos like Lennon & McCartney, Rodgers & Hammerstein, Bacharach & David, Goffin & King, Lerner & Loewe, and on and on and on, have found great success working as a team.

Songwriting collaborations often involve one individual writing the music and the other writing the lyrics. But what about collaborations for instrumental music? Does one person write the melody while the other writes the chords? Let's look at some scenarios and find out why collaboration may be beneficial for you.

Productivity

Writing with another individual can help you generate more music. It can increase your output by 2 to 3 times what you might produce yourself. By splitting duties, you can be more productive than working solo. Working with a collaborator forces you to follow through on your commitments. By depending on one another collaborators feel a sense of obligation to not disappoint each other.

Writing a cue is not the only thing you do. Mixing, mastering, creating stems and metadata...all of these things take time. You can work on the next cue while your collaborator is doing the mixes. Later your collaborator can compose their parts while you take over on some of the other duties. Treat it like a factory assembly line.

Spark Creativity

You may get stuck and experience writer's block. A collaborator can suggest a solution or jump in and take over the reins. A suggestion by your collaborator can send you in a new direction. This new direction might result in a much better cue than originally designed, or could trigger an idea for yet *another* cue. Boom! You've just created two cues instead of one.

Be open and bounce ideas off one another. After a while a collaboration partnership becomes like a marriage: Knowing in advance what the other person is thinking; Knowing how to resolve problems that arise during the creative process.

Improve Your Skills

Working with another person can often lead to improved skills, both technical and creative. Seeing how someone else approaches something can be both informative and enlightening. Not everybody does the things you do the same way. Embrace this gift.

Share Duties

There are many ways to collaborate. One writer can come up with a chord progression and a groove while the other writer comes up with a killer melody. Consider splitting up composing sections of the cue. For example, one writer composes the A section and the other composes the B section.

When composing alone, we use the same internal thought process when developing the 'B' section resulting in cues that sound "just like the last one". Having your collaborator create the B section takes you in a direction you never would have on your own. This may cause a fresh perspective that might not have been achieved if written by a single composer.

Non-composing Collaborations

Not all collaborations are compositional in nature. A valid collaboration can be anything from one person composing the music while the collaborator contributes by mixing the track, or performs some of instrumental parts. Even having one person handling clerical duties such a creating metadata and file uploads can warrant a collaboration split.

How to Find Collaborators

The great thing about the world we live in today is that it's smaller. And by smaller, I mean that someone across the globe is no farther than someone living down the street from you. Thanks to the Internet it's possible to collaborate with anyone, anywhere in the world.

> *"Most of them I have met and learned to know at music conferences or via the Internet on online forums and such. I focus on collaborating with people I trust, who have proven themselves as a friend, quality musician, and ethical businessperson."* - **Lydia Ashton, composer**

So where do you find collaborators? Living in areas such as Los Angeles, New York, Chicago, and Nashville, you had better chances of finding many candidates to collaborate with. But we are no longer limited to these large metropolitan areas anymore. We can find collaborators online, anywhere on the globe.

Websites such as www.kompoz.com, forums.taxi.com, and www.cocompose.com, and even Facebook and LinkedIn groups offer ways to find people to work with. Some of these sites can be like online dating. You'll want to get to know people by their previous work before deciding if they would make good partners. There should be mutual respect between you. You don't want to get into a situation where you feel you're carrying most of the load. It needs to be a team effort.

Music departments at local colleges is another a great way to find like-minded composers. If you belong to any songwriter or composer organizations, they usually offer some type of service to hook people up looking to collaborate.

Working online with your collaborator can be a lot like playing chess-by-mail. You make a move and wait for you opponent (or collaborator in this case) to make theirs. This can mean waiting several days before getting a response and a chance to add your input. Try to find other things you can work on while waiting for your collaborator to get back to you - working on additional material or even the next cue so you're never without something to do.

If your collaborator is in a far geographical location, this can mean that while you're asleep they are working on their part and vice-versa. This keeps the momentum going. It also motivates you to have something ready for your collaborator, otherwise they will be very bored when their turn comes!

Scheduling Time

When composing on your own you will work whenever the time is convenient to you. When working with collaborators, however, you are now in a situation to set up a schedule that works for both of you. As mentioned above, if you're working in different time zones you want to schedule your hours so they flow with your partner's. Having your collaborator wait can lead to resentment. Try to establish reasonable expectations.

If you know you need several days to accomplish a task, make sure you let your collaborator know ahead of time. Don't leave them guessing. Things come up. Everybody understands that life happens. Keep the communication lines open. Sounds like a marriage, right? It is no different. People are people and you must respect each other.

Legal Agreements

Before you do anything with a collaborator, be sure you've discussed and *signed* an agreement between the two of you. I can't stress this enough. You may be the best of friends, but that's how friendships are destroyed. Outline how you are splitting ownership of the composition(s).

IMPORTANT: One of the collaborators must be able to speak on behalf of the rest of the team. If a publisher asks you if the music is free and clear you must be able to answer that question. When a publisher has an opportunity for placing your music they need to know you can give them a definitive answer. Don't put them in an awkward position by saying, "Let me ask my writing partner if this is okay"! You will most likely lose out on the opportunity because the publisher can't wait.

You can either create a separate written agreement for each composition you work on, or create an agreement that includes *any and all* compositions you work on together. Why a written agreement? Isn't a handshake just as good? More friendships have been destroyed because both parties have different memories of what was agreed upon. A written agreement, or contract, lays out in black-and-white the terms of the agreement. It doesn't have to be drawn up by a lawyer, but at the very least have it notarized.

> *"Handshake agreements are not a good idea because there are no clearly defined terms in writing and disputes then become a "he-said/she-said" scenario. It is best to have all terms clearly defined so there is less chance of misinterpretation later." - **Erin M. Jacobson, music attorney**

What's fair? Agree to split everything 50/50. Especially if you will work together more than a single time. There is no way to calculate how much contribution each party made. Sometimes you'll do more of the work and sometimes your collaborator will. In the long run, it all evens out. If you find your collaborator is barely contributing then you can stop working with them. It happens.

You must make this agreement *before* you begin. If you try to do it after-the-fact, you will never agree that "composer A did 70% of the work and composer B did only 30%". It's not worth arguing over.

We'll discuss more about contracts in *Chapter 21 - Contracts and Other Legal Stuff.*

Working out Artistic Disagreements

Having disagreements about creative work is inevitable. Being human, we all have opinions. Some of us express them in stronger ways than others. We said earlier that collaborations are like any partnership, or even a marriage. Disagreements will occur from time to time.

How do we handle these creative disagreements? Should one partner take the lead and always have the final say? If that's what you agree upon up-front, then okay. Otherwise, you must compromise. Be open-minded. Your collaborator may suggest something you never considered. Try it. Even if you disagree, allow your collaborator a "win". It's all give-and-take.

Try to learn from your experiences. Using a sports analogy, go back over the "game tape" later on and see if what your collaborator suggested was the right thing. It's easier to be objective after time has passed.

Conflict can be a good thing. Try to leverage the emotional discomfort by using it to create more ideas. We all have egos, and sometimes it's better to let go of it for the sake of teamwork.

As they say, "two heads are better than one"! Try collaboration, you may like the results.

Chapter 11 _____

QUALITY VS QUANTITY

"If you're not making mistakes, then you're not doing anything. I'm positive that a doer makes mistakes." - **John Wooden**

Why Quantity?

To make money writing production music for TV you must have lots and lots of cues in music catalogs. But not just *in* the music catalogs - those cues need to get *placed*. It's safe to say less than 100% of your cues in these music catalogs will ever see a placement in a TV show. It's not because any of those cues are bad, it's just that those cues didn't fit any opportunities.

You need to write A LOT of music. **Quantity** is a very important factor here. How many cues are enough? 100? 500? 1,000? 5,000??? There is no magic number. Being a writer of production music follows the 80/20 rule in business: 80% of your income will derive from 20% of your work. It's true. You'll have tracks that get used over and over and over again. Some of your tracks will get used a few times - sometimes just once. And still others will never get used. Ever.

Production music is a numbers game. Music libraries themselves work in the same way. They need lots and lots of tracks in their catalogs to succeed. The more music you have available the better your chances of success. What you need is a targeted strategy.

How do you target your music? By understanding what the industry wants. You can produce hundreds of tracks of polka music, but unless there are a lot of shows about Oktoberfest, you might not find many opportunities for that kind of music. Be smart about the music you write. Once you determine what is in demand, write lots and lots of it!

*"I only have quality in mind. I've gotten to a point where I have a reputation for quality that every project that I do there are high expectations from the clients, so that I will deliver top-notch quality. That's the only thing I focus on." - **Matt Hirt, composer**

Why Quality?

How much music can you produce over a period of a year, a month, a week, a day? If you can produce 10 or more tracks in a day, it's likely that the quality of the music is sub-par. Why? It means you're taking too many shortcuts.

Sure it's possible to create numerous solo piano or solo acoustic guitar tracks over the course of a single day. But what about any ensemble piece, such as an orchestral cue, or even a Hip Hop track? Those cues involve many instrument parts. If you're working with MIDI tracks involving different sampled instruments, you know it takes time to program the parts with CC controller data to produce natural articulations for each instrument. Without spending the time to do this properly you'll end up with tracks that sound "too MIDI".

Another shortcut is in the mixing process. Mixing the instrument levels, or having sounds that battle a particular frequency range will ruin an otherwise perfectly good track. Mixing takes time. The more instruments to mix, the more difficult and time-consuming it becomes.

The lower the quality of your tracks, the worse your chances are of finding placements for these cues. In this case, it doesn't matter if you produce one million tracks per year.

*"Early on I tried to get as many pieces as possible out there, and didn't always take the time to polish my music. After a couple of years in the business I learned that the polished, well produced pieces got better placements, and thus earned me more money." - **Lydia Ashton, composer**

———————————————————————

Tips for Achieving Both

Your goal is to produce a maximum number of tracks each year while maintaining a level of quality that will result in lots of placements. After working for a while you'll know how many tracks you can produce regularly. Next, you'll want to improve this output by *any* factor. Even an increase of 10% will benefit you.

> *"The thing we look for the most in a composer is the ability to deliver fully mixed and flawless tracks ready for mastering and delivery."*
> **- Jeff Rona, Liquid Cinema**

As discussed in *Chapter 8 - The Composing Process,* working from templates will get you going that much faster. By having specific templates for each style, you write in will help keep you focused on the composing process and less about the technical parts.

Also in Chapter 8 we talked about using other people's music as a "musical template". This was a way to understand the structure and form of a composition and integrate your own personal touch. But instead of using other people's music, why not use *your own* music as a template?

By taking your own existing track, replace the melody over the same chord progression. Change the key and tempo to give it a different sound. By virtue of the acoustical properties of Western music, the overtone series of various scales take on a whole new texture simply by changing the key signature. Besides changing the key and tempo, replace some of the instrumentation. You can create a brand-new piece of music with minimal effort.

If you are a songwriter, that is, songs with lyrics, plan on creating an instrumental version of the cue. Replace the vocals with a melody instrument. You have now doubled your cue count by creating this instrumental version.

When given a choice between writing quality cues or writing a large quantity of cues of marginal quality, choose quality. Your return on investment will be higher in the long run.

*"If you're pitching to the trailer market, those standards are very high. If the intended usage is more for background you can probably get away with more sampled sounds than not. People are expecting to hear music that doesn't call attention to itself. If the sounds don't sound right, people will notice it." - **Edwina Travis-Chin, APM Music***

Chapter 12 _____

MANAGING YOUR TIME

"Don't let making a living prevent you from making a life." - **John Wooden**

Music as a Full-Time Job

Is music your full-time job? It's okay to say no. When I say full-time, I mean you earn enough money from writing music or other music activities to support yourself and your loved ones. This includes paying a mortgage if you own your own home, or paying rent if you live in an apartment. It also refers to covering the cost of living: food, health insurance, utilities, karate lessons. Whatever it includes, are you covering it with your music work?

It can take a while to get to that point. For production music composers, it will take a *minimum* of 5 years to reach that point. You may have other music-related income to support you as well: performing in bands, teaching, recording engineer, church musician, session musician, singer. If you've made music a way of life, congratulations! Music can be one of the most rewarding jobs a person can have.

But suppose you want to shift your energy from these other music-related jobs and focus on becoming a composer writing music for TV. You must consider all of the tasks that go into the job of "TV Music Composer".

The job description of "TV Music Composer" is not "Write music, get paid, buy yacht". In fact, the actual composing part of the job is a tiny part of what you'll be doing. Sorry to disappoint you. The tasks included in this job consist of:

- **Research**
  Find out what music is being sought after. Learning new styles. Learning new production skills. Learning software.

- **Composing the Music**

The fun part!

- **Recording the Cue**

Playing each instrument and/or recording musicians playing their parts.

- **Mixing the Cue**

Doing the work of an engineer. Includes the mastering process.

- **Creating Stems**

These are the various versions of the cue. A lot of thought goes into deciding what to include in each stem. Every cue is different.

- **Exporting Audio**

Creating MP3's, AIFF's, WAV's, or whatever format that is required.

- **Generating Metadata**

The boring part. Find appropriate keywords and other descriptive information about each cue.

- **Communicating with Collaborators (if applicable)**

Working with your collaborator(s) via email, phone, or Skype (video conferencing). Uploading and/or downloading works-in-progress.

- **Uploading the Cue**

Upload or submit the audio files and metadata via whatever protocol the music library has instructed you to use.

- **Update Cataloging Software**

This is a recordkeeping task so you'll have this important information at your fingertips when someone asks you for a certain kind of cue, you'll know where to find it.

- **Backing Up Your Data**

Making sure all of your hard work has been backed up locally and off-site (the cloud).

- **Answering Email and Phone Calls**

Handle all of the email correspondence for the day and returning phone calls.

- **Sales Calls**

Also email and telephone, contacting potential clients.

- **Creating and Submitting Demos**

Sending out demos - either CDs via regular mail or uploading music (mp3s) to streaming sites.

- **Networking**

Attending industry events such as seminars and screenings; Meeting colleagues and potential clients.

These are all tasks that need to be addressed on a daily basis. If any of them fall through the cracks, you may see a drop in revenue as a result. If you're successful enough you can hire an assistant (or two) to handle some of the more mundane tasks. But if your assistant is not a recording engineer, you may need to hire one of those as well.

Music as a Part-Time Job

As you can see from the list above, there are quite a few tasks involved when writing music for TV. In fact, it often feels like an 8-hour work day is not enough to handle all of the tasks.

So, what do you do if you're trying to do this part-time? Many composers *have* succeeded while holding down a day job to support themselves and their family. It's not impossible! You need to manage your time differently - but effectively.

As we'll see next, when your time is limited you will need to plan a schedule that meets the demands of your day job and your home life. This can be challenging, and probably a little frustrating. Setting up a schedule you adhere to will help you stay focused.

> "With the resources available today it wouldn't take as long for someone to become a full-time composer as it did for us"
> - *Tracey & Vance Marino, composers*

Scheduling: Business and Creative

Being a production music composer is more than just writing music. As we saw from the tasks above there are quite a few business-related items on the list. As much as we'd like to just focus on writing music, if we don't address the business activities we won't be able to advance our careers.

We need to separate the business side from the creative side. Since it's likely that you'll be doing all of this yourself (without help) it's important to understand how to schedule your time effectively. How we schedule these tasks depend on whether we are doing this full time or part time.

Full Time Composers

Let assume you'll be working an 8-hour day / 5-day week.

—————————————————————————

Sometimes you must put in more hours on any given day and work on weekends, but let's consider this an extreme case. We'll also assume that you're working on creating new cues every day. This is not for any special project nor just goofing around. This schedule is based on the idea that you are a music factory, cranking out one cue after another fulfilling the needs of music buyers.

Your office/studio setup should be free of distractions. No radio, no television, no washing machines, and no social media (Facebook, Twitter, Instagram, etc.). You need to be disciplined and focus on your work. This is a job. If the boss finds out you're goofing around you'll get fired!

Get the business activities out of the way first. That means handling email correspondence, phone calls, mailing out demos. Any activity that relates to the promotion of your business. Limit yourself to an hour or two at the most. This limit forces you to get the work done. Your reward is getting back to your music writing! Also, don't look at email throughout the day. This will distract you and sidetrack you for hours. I especially recommend *NOT* spending time with social media while you're trying to work. I know this is hard. Going down this rabbit hole can suck away valuable hours out of your life!

The rest of your day should be focused on creating music: Composing the music and performing the parts. Beyond that, the rest of the work that relates to completing a music cue is not creative. The mixing, mastering, creating stems, logging cues, data backup, metadata creation, etc. This is where you have a couple of options.

If you're just working on one cue at a time, it's best to work from start to finish: Record the music followed by the clerical work. But if you're doing a project, for example, producing 10 cues for a particular music library catalog request. Here, you might find it more efficient to group the tasks. Compose all 10 tracks and record the parts; then mix all 10 tracks; then create stems for all 10 tracks; then log all 10 cues in your database;

then backup data for all 10 cues, etc.

The reason for this is so your brain can focus on one activity at a time. Switching back and forth between various left- and right-brain functions can be extremely fatiguing.

Part Time Composers

How many hours each day can you allocate to work on music? Ideally, you'd like to have at least two hours a day. After working a full day, coming home, eating dinner, spending time with the family, doing chores...it doesn't leave much time, does it?

More than anything else, being consistent is the key. Even if this means only finding two hours *per week!* Let's take a look at a schedule assuming you have about 2 hours a day (5 days a week) to do this.

Like the schedule above for full timers, plan on dealing with email and phone calls first. That may mean spending all 2 hours on Monday doing this and leaving the rest of the week to do the actual music work. But you're thinking, "I can't afford to give up one of my five days to deal with business stuff. My time is so limited!" If you don't take care of *any* business, whatever you do creatively will go nowhere. This is an important path to success.

If your day job is in the daytime hours (8 am - 6 pm), you will find it difficult to make phone calls in the evening. If you can't set aside some time, perhaps during your lunch hour to make phone calls, stick to email. In fact, most clients prefer email as the de facto communication method anyway.

The same suggestions apply regarding the order of tasks as the full timers. Complete a cue (composition and clerical work) before moving on to the next cue - unless you're working on a project.

Work/Life Balance

Finding the right balance between work and life is often challenging.

If you have a family, it's important to make time for them. Life is short. Even when you feel like the only way you'll get things done is to work late into the night and all weekend long.

By spending all your time working you will not only alienate the people around you, your quality of work will suffer by virtue of fatigue. Studies have shown that productivity dips exponentially as your amount of time working increases. This is called "burn out" (not a technical term). Step away from your work when you're tired and come back when you're rested.

The work/life balance is challenging for those trying to do this on a part-time basis. You can still achieve a huge amount of success, albeit at a slower pace. I've seen this with many individuals. Many of them have transitioned from part-time to full-time. It can happen.

> *"There is no one perfect path that works for everyone. What are you willing to give up to have the career you want? What would you be willing to give up to keep your family?"* - **Lydia Ashton, composer**

Part 3

Technical Aspects

Chapter 13 _____

RECORDING YOUR MUSIC

"The key to longevity is to learn every aspect of music that you can." - **Prince**

Traditional Recording Studios

You may be old enough to remember there was a time when you needed something other than a computer to record music with. In the "old" days you would have to go somewhere, a professional recording studio of some sort, to record your music. Not only that, every musical instrument - *real* musical instruments - would be performed by musicians. Ah, the good old days.

Traditional recording studios still exist. Maybe not in the same grand sense. Studios are now in homes, garages, warehouses, office spaces, barns, and churches. The only real difference is that tape recorders have been replaced with computers. The basic concept of recording real instruments with microphones has not changed.

Most production music composers are self-contained. They record everything "in the box". That means that most musical instruments will be virtual instruments, that is, digitally sampled instruments. While this is common practice, there is a great benefit to recording actual instruments on your tracks. Adding *any* real instruments to your digital instruments will add just enough realism to fool the ear into thinking *everything* is real.

I'll emphasize this again: Any opportunity you have to add real instruments to your recordings you will increase your chances of music placements by a significant percentage. The curse of using virtual instruments is having your tracks labeled as sounding *"too MIDI"*.

You need not have a full-fledged recording studio to record real instruments. Having a real recording studio would be really, really cool, but it's unnecessary. To record real instruments, you need just a few items:

- **Microphones**

Depending on the instruments you are recording you can get by with just a few mics: a dynamic mic such as a Shure SM57 or 58 (inexpensive); a large diaphragm condenser mic such as a Neumann u87 (expensive) or a Gauge ECM-87 (inexpensive); or a small diaphragm condenser mic such as a Shure SM81 (moderately priced) or the AKG C 451 B (a bit more than the Shure). There are too many great mics to list here.

- **Mic stands**

Microphone stands are very inexpensive. Most are tripods, but some feature a heavy single-leg base. Boom extensions are often necessary when recording drums.

- **Mic cables**

Good quality mic cables are important. The sound quality can vary when using low quality cables. Better to spend more for these.

- **Sound treatment**

Depending on the size and layout of your room, you'll get better sound results with moderate placement of sound treatment, particularly bass traps.

- **Recording interface**

You'll need to get audio instruments (microphone or guitar cable) into your computer. A USB audio interface is the way to go. Configurations range from a single input up to 8 inputs. If you need more inputs, just add more interfaces.

- **Headphones**

This is one item where quality counts. Sometimes you must mix using headphones only, especially for those living in apartments. Headphones with a flat frequency response will give you the best results.

MIDI keyboard

You can achieve great results with the simplest keyboard, as long as it functions as a MIDI controller. Most of your work will deal with virtual instruments and the most common way of entering data (musical notes) is with a MIDI keyboard.

Recording "In the Box"

One item *not* listed above is your computer. Although there are a few die-hards still using tape recorders, most of the rest of the world are using computers to record their music. Recording "in the box" means that everything is done with your computer using software designed for recording music. These "digital audio workstations" (DAW) are the cornerstone of music production.

Since most everyone already owns a computer of some sort, you are already most of the way there with what it takes to create music. Whether you are using a PC or Mac, you will be able to produce professional-sounding music tracks. It almost doesn't matter which DAW you use. It's a level playing field. Most DAWs do the same things and have the same or similar features - even if they achieve the results in different ways. Popular DAWs include: Sonar (PC only), Logic Pro (Mac only), Cubase, Pro Tools, Digital Performer, FL Studio, and Ableton Live. These are among the most popular used by professionals, but there are several others to consider.

Which is the *best* DAW? It's the one you're used to. I mean this sincerely. They are all so close in features it almost makes no difference. But do the research. Some have stronger MIDI-editing capabilities, while some - like Pro Tools - have become the de facto standard with professional recording studios.

Minimal Equipment

If you're just starting out, what is the minimum amount of equipment you need to produce music? First, a computer. It's likely you already have that. If you don't own one, you must decide on a Mac or a PC. Macs are pricier than PCs. There are many different brands of PCs available, including being able to build one yourself. This competition results in low prices. Macs are proprietary hardware and come with a hefty price tag. While Mac users hate PCs with a passion and most PC users don't understand Macs, let me say I own and use both. Like DAW features we discussed, computer capabilities on these two platforms are comparable.

Later on we'll discuss using slave computers and you'll see why you'll most likely be using PCs for those even if you are a Mac user.

A MIDI keyboard is almost a necessity. It *is* possible to enter MIDI data from your computer keyboard or draw in notes with a mouse, but it is much easier to use a MIDI keyboard even if you don't know how to play a piano. MIDI recording software allows you to "step" enter notes one at a time. It couldn't be easier.

You'll need a MIDI/audio interface to connect analog instruments such as guitars and microphones as well as connecting your MIDI keyboard. Today, these are USB devices although some Firewire boxes still exist. The most basic interfaces can cost as low as $50.

USB Audio Interfaces

Figure 13-1

Figure 13-2

To hear the music, you should have speakers. Quality ones can be expensive, so until you're ready to make that investment you'll want to get headphones. As we discussed earlier, a quality pair is the next best thing to having good speakers.

Your computer can even be a laptop. Many composers have been extremely portable with their production studio, producing tracks while even flying on an airplane! A laptop, a pair of headphones, and a portable MIDI keyboard will all fit in a backpack. Have music will travel!

Sound Treatment

Most of us don't have a professionally designed and acoustically optimal recording space. In fact, most self-contained production music composers work in a small space like a spare bedroom.

When we talk about sound treatment we are not referring to *soundproofing*. This is a subject for double-wall construction techniques and beyond the scope of this book. The sound treatment I'm referring to is methods for *controlling* the frequencies in your sound space. The room you're working in contains six surfaces: a ceiling, a floor, and four walls. All of these surfaces are very reflective and sound will bounce around your room like a pinball machine.

Low frequencies are non-directional as opposed to higher frequencies that fly around in straight lines. The low frequencies congregate in the corners of your room. This issue is solved by using *bass traps*. These are big pieces of foam that fit in the corner where the walls meet.

Dealing with the higher frequencies are more challenging. So, unless you will cover 100% of your walls, floor, and ceiling with absorbent material, you must be smart about treating the room. With no significant frequency analysis, it's recommended at the least to set up treatment directly behind

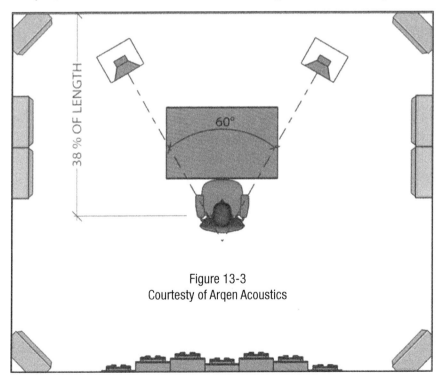

Figure 13-3
Courtesty of Arqen Acoustics

you, directly in front of you (behind your speakers), on the left- and right-walls directly in-line with your ears, and directly above you on the ceiling. Beyond that, you must do some experimenting to find out where the live spots are in your space.

Typical sound treatment solutions include foam panels by companies such as Auralex and Arqen Acoustics. There are many companies now that make these panels. Auralex was one of the first professional/consumer products on the market. You can also build your own if you are handy enough.

Software: DAWS and Plugins

Your DAW (Digital Audio Workstation), is "command central" in your world. This is where you record, edit, mix, tweak, and playback your music tracks. You *can* attach the computer to outboard FX (compressors, limiters, reverbs, etc.) and even a mixing console, but a majority of composers will do their work within the computing environment. There's a very good reason for this: All of your FX settings, volume levels, panning positions, bus assignments, etc. are saved with your project. In fact, some DAWs allow you to save "snapshots" of various mixes to instantly recall a mix and to compare it with other mixes. A/B alternate mixes with ease!

As I said earlier, most DAWs today are similar in features. Before digital audio recording was common, these DAWs were referred to as *sequencers*. Their sole purpose was recording MIDI data to multiple tracks. Many were limited to only 16 channels of MIDI data. Each track triggered sounds on hardware synthesizers and samplers connected via a MIDI cable. Turning this MIDI data into audio required capturing the audio from the sound card in your computer and routing any external sound sources and mixing it to a DAT (Digital Audio Tape) recorder, reel-to-reel, or cassette tape. Archaic by today's standards.

All of the sounds you could ever need can be run within your DAW environment on your computer. You are only limited by CPU speed,

RAM, and hard drive speeds. The more power you have the more you can accomplish. Computers are currently configured with 16-, 32-, 64-, and even 128-GB RAM. Hard drives are being replaced by even more affordable and super-fast solid-state drives (SSD).

The need for external hardware synthesizers and samplers have been replaced by software *plugins*. Some years ago a digital audio software sampler called *Gigastudio* broke the barrier of hardware samplers by allowing samples of unlimited size (limited only by your RAM). Sadly, this innovative program is no longer available. Today, most music production composers have switched over to Native Instrument's *Kontakt* sample player. This popular tool is available and compatible with most DAWs on both PC and Mac platforms. Other popular sample players include EastWest's *PLAY engine,* and *VSL's Vienna Instruments Player.*

There are hundreds (maybe thousands) of virtual instruments available for the Kontakt player. Both PLAY and the Vienna Instruments platforms are limited to virtual instruments developed by their respective companies. In terms of flexibility and diversity, the Kontakt player has the most options with virtual instrument libraries developed by many companies.

If you're on a limited budget there are options to consider since owning just a few of these virtual instrument libraries can add up to several thousand dollars. Native Instruments offers *Kontakt Komplete* and *Kontakt Komplete Ultimate* bundles. These bundles include hundreds of virtual instruments running the gamut from orchestral instruments, band instruments, pianos, guitars, basses, drums, and synthesizers and sound design instruments of every imaginable type.

Alternatively, EastWest (at the time of this writing) has been offering the ability to "rent" everything in their catalog for a monthly fee. This gives you access to what would cost you tens of thousands of dollars if you were to purchase each of these libraries. The caveat here is that once you stop paying the monthly subscription you no longer have access to the sounds. We will discuss how to deal with this scenario in *Chapter 17 - Backing Up Your Tracks.*

Virtual instruments are not the only thing DAW plugins are good for. Sound processing plugins include mixing and mastering tools such as compressors, limiters, convolution reverbs, delays, flangers, chorus...the list is endless. You can even plug in a guitar and use amplifier simulator plugins to emulate the sound of classic guitar amps.

DAWs and plugins have changed the way composers work. The ability to be self-contained has opened the doors to producing some amazing music cues.

Slave Computers

An unfortunate metaphor, a "slave" computer is a computer that is controlled by a "master" computer. What this means in the world of music production, you can use the computing power of an unlimited number of devices (slaves) to increase your instrument voice count.

An amazing piece of programming design has resulted in VSL's *Vienna Ensemble Pro* (aka VE PRO) instrument routing software. Installing a VE Pro Server on your DAW and each slave computer allows the DAW to communicate with the slave's VE Pro via an Ethernet cable that is already part of your Internet network. A home Wi-Fi router is all you need to configure these servers. See figure 13-4.

A VE Pro server will allow you to install numerous virtual instruments, e.g. Kontakt instruments, that can be selected by your DAW as if the instrument was loaded on the DAW's computer. It's an amazing feat to know digital audio is being transmitted across a normal computer networking cable.

To employ multiple slave computers, the most common approach is to use PC hardware due to its low cost (as compared to Macs). Multiple computers can take advantage of KVM (keyboard-video-mouse) switches to share a single keyboard, video monitor, and mouse.

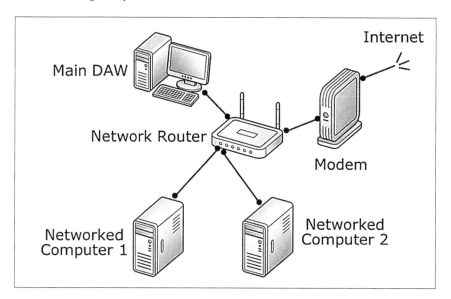

Figure 13-4

Templates

We discussed in *Chapter 8 - The Composing Process*, the use of templates in your DAW. By spending time building these templates you will increase your productivity. As you can see from the availability of sound processing plugins you can preconfigure tracks, buses, and instrument plugins customized to the music you are creating.

What makes templates even more useful is having the instrument tracks pointing to plugins that have been preloaded on slave computers via VE Pro. This speeds up the load time when opening a project. The virtual instrument plugins don't have to load every instrument in your template. The only loading involved is for unique instruments that apply to that specific project. Fill up your slave computers with instruments you use daily - such as orchestral instruments - and save the DAW project for those occasional instruments.

CHAPTER 13

Getting Started

If you're just starting out you need not spend more than you can afford to produce great sounding tracks. I didn't mention *Garage Band*, the free music recording app that comes with Mac and iOS devices, as a DAW option. This is not considered a professional tool for music production. But if you're just starting out and this is all you have, then use it! It's not a bad tool, it's just limited compared to what is available in higher end DAWs.

Also, as mentioned before, use live musical instruments whenever possible. This will add value particularly if your virtual instruments are less than optimal. Don't fall into the trap of believing *"if only I had <fill in the blank> my music would be awesome"*. Your music is already awesome. It's what's in your heart, not what's in your computer.

Chapter 14 _____

USING SAMPLE LIBRARIES

"It's not so much a necessity as it is an addiction." - **Matt Hirt**

What Are Sample Libraries?

We've come a long way in electronic musical instruments and synthesis. From the Theremin in 1920, the Ondes Martenot in 1928, the Clavivox synthesizer in 1956, the Minimoog in 1970, the Prophet-5 in 1977, and the DX-7 in 1983. All of these produced invented - synthesized - sounds. Digital sampling - the recording and rendering of actual instrument sounds - saw the Synclavier in 1977, the Fairlight CMI in 1978, the Kurzweil K250 in 1983, the E-mu Emulator III (also 1983), and the Akai S900 in 1986. The digital sampling industry never looked back.

> *"It has to sound realistic. Your composition might be the most amazing composition on earth, but if it does not sound good (realistic) it will never be used."* - **Lydia Ashton, composer**

One of the most popular samplers on the market was the Akai S1000 (1988) which introduced 16-bit sampling. It offered RAM that could be expanded to a whopping 32 MB! It could load a single instrument and had a polyphonic limit of 16 voices. Composers needed racks of these samplers to create music scores. The cost of these setups could topple $50,000.

If you're just entering the world of sampled musical instruments, you arrived at a great time. Today your investment is a small fraction of what you would have needed to spend in the early 1990's. And what you get for that smaller investment is at least *10 times* what you would have gotten back then. We are truly living in a modern world.

While today's samplers such as *Kontakt* support recording your own samples and building custom instruments, most composers treat these tools as sample *players*, meaning that off-the-shelf sample libraries are loaded into the player and played as-is. There is nothing wrong with this. There are so many incredible sample libraries out there that you would be hard pressed to be *un*able to find the exact sounds you are looking for.

In those pioneering years of sampling you would have needed racks of samplers. Today's software samplers use this same metaphor. Multiple instruments can be loaded into a single instance of Kontakt. Additional instances of Kontakt can be opened to load even more instruments. You are only limited by available memory in your computer.

The example below (figure 14-1) shows a Kontakt player with several instruments loaded in racks in the right pane. The last instrument in the list at the bottom of the rack has been expanded to reveal a set of controls specific to that instrument.

Figure 14-1

The left pane of the Kontakt player displays all of the samples libraries you have installed on your computer. Each sample library comes with one or more "instruments". Loading an instrument adds it to the rack pane on the right. Each instrument is assigned a MIDI channel (1-16). Multiple instruments can be assigned the same MIDI channel. In this way, you can layer sounds by having each one respond to the same MIDI channel for every note you play. You can save these custom configurations as "multis". Instead of loading individual instruments and rebuilding your layered instruments, you can load a multi and all of the instruments will be loaded automatically.

Figure 14-2

In the next example (figure 14-2), two other instruments have been expanded revealing a unique interface. These interfaces include parameters that only make sense to this particular instrument. The same parameters may or may not be relevant in any other instrument. The interfaces are visually stunning making the user experience very satisfying.

The custom configurations used in today's sampled instruments could never be accomplished with early hardware samplers. Those samplers required a basic set of functions and were limited to strictly those. Later models introduced software driven interfaces displayed on a tiny screen - better but still limited. This was a precursor to what you are seeing today.

One more example (figure 14-3) shows the EastWest PLAY interface. Like the interfaces in Kontakt sample libraries each interface is configured for that particular library. In this example, the EastWest/Quantum Leap Symphonic Orchestra is displayed.

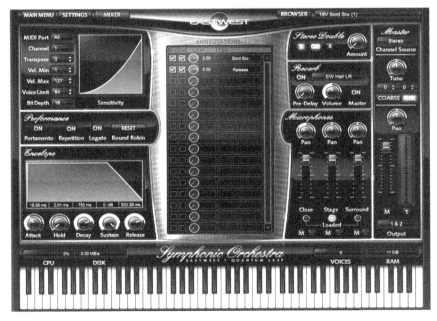

Figure 14-3

How to Choose the Right Ones

With so many choices on the market for sample libraries, which are the right ones for you? Guessing the correct lottery numbers might be an easier question to answer. The simplest answer is, *it depends*.

First, let's start with budget. If you're just starting out you may not have an unlimited budget. Most of us don't. You need to be smart about your selections. What kind of music are you creating? If you are limiting your work to just a few but similar genres, you might get away with just a few related libraries. But if you're planning on dipping your feet into an ocean of styles, you'll need something more flexible and diverse.

> *"The only sounds you would want to stay current on is realistic emulations of real instruments because that technology just keeps getting better. You can't get by with something that's 10 years old anymore because the standards have gone up."* - **Matt Hirt, composer**

I'm hesitant to be specific about sample libraries on the market today. Newer libraries are introduced every 6 months and it's possible that by the time you are reading this book, any libraries mentioned here may not be available anymore, have been updated, or replacement libraries have taken their places.

With that said, I will mention many of the companies making these libraries as they are likely to be around for a while even if specific libraries they make today may not be around down the line. I will mention once again Native Instrument's *Kontakt Komplete (or Komplete Ultimate)* bundles. These bundles are so diverse you are likely to get by with these sounds for quite a long time. At the time of this writing, Komplete is around $600 USD and Komplete Ultimate is around $1,200 USD. By comparison, you can spend $500-$800 USD just for an orchestral strings library. There are reasons you would want to upgrade to some of the higher priced libraries, and no doubt you will as your business grows.

For a list of companies creating sample libraries, refer to *Appendix C: Sample Library Companies*. This list does *not* contain looping libraries. *Loops* falls into a different category than sample libraries. They are not customizable the way sampled instruments are. Our focus in this chapter is on sample libraries.

Customize or Stock?

Can you load an instrument from a sample library and play it or do you need to tweak the parameters to make any sounds? Synthesized instruments (as opposed to sampled instruments based on actual instruments such as a guitar or oboe) require a great deal of programming to make sounds. These instruments may come with a catalog of pre-programmed sounds, but you will adjust parameters to make sounds tailored to your needs.

With sampled instruments such as orchestral or band, they will sound just fine right out of the box. This is great because you want to be productive as quickly as possible. You may not need to change the sound by adjusting EQ or the envelope by adjusting ADSR, but you may wish to customize the acoustical environment by adding convolution reverbs or adjusting the panning to place the instrument in a different virtual spot on the stage.

Standing Out Above the Crowd

Should you change the sound of an instrument? If you're using traditional orchestral instruments (strings, woodwinds, brass, percussion) then it's likely that these instruments need to sound exactly like orchestral instruments. But if you're using non-traditional instruments then there is no bar to measure what the instruments should sound like. Tweak the sounds until you find something that works for you.

"My measure whether I should buy something has been, 'Will this simplify working on this project?' or, 'Will this library greatly improve my sound?' or, 'Are the samples easier to make sound realistic than what I currently work with?'" - **Lydia Ashton, composer**

There is also a reason to *always* tweak non-traditional instruments to sound unique. You want to sound different than everybody else. There is nothing worse for music supervisors than hearing the same stock sounds. Their reaction might be something like *"I guess everybody bought library XYZ this week!"* You want to stand out above the crowd. You want to have a unique signature, something that no one else is doing. This journey is often referred to as "finding your voice".

But there is also a reason to tweak traditional instrument sounds. With orchestral instruments, the bar is very, very high these days. Your strings must sound exactly like real strings. Woodwinds must sound exactly like real woodwinds. If your sounds are sub-par your tracks will be labeled as sounding "too MIDI". Until you can afford to improve your sample libraries you should consider modifying the sounds, even layering sounds, until you come up with something that is unique and still works within the context of the style of music you're writing.

Hopefully you'll be able to stay updated with all of the great new libraries as they are introduced throughout the year. But don't feel pressure to purchase libraries you can't afford. Work with what you've got until your business has grown enough to warrant expanding your sound library. It may be a slow process, but it will be worth it.

Your New Sample Library

If you're like me, every time a new sample library is introduced you are tempted to buy it and add to your collection. What's even worse is when every sample library company offers deep discounts on their products - especially around Christmas time. You may buy several new libraries. Way to go!

As great as this sounds, you might find yourself overwhelmed with these new libraries, their vast capabilities and how to use them. If you have purchased additional libraries from a company with products you already own, you will notice similar interfaces and common programming paradigms within their product line. But if this is the first time using a product by this particular company you might be a little lost.

Don't expect to just load in an instrument into a project and hear amazing sounds right out of the box. There will be a learning curve to get it to sound like the demos you heard and which convinced you to buy the product. Without taking the time to learn the new instrument you will waste valuable creative time and could put your project in jeopardy if you are facing a deadline.

> *"When we buy a new package of software I will take an entire afternoon and go through every single patch and I'll make notes on it."*
> *- Tracey & Vance Marino, composers*

Exploration

Block out time to learn the instrument. Find out what sounds are included. Understand how to program any configurable settings. Determine if you can control any sounds with CC controller data. Often these instruments give you multiple ways to do something, such as switching samples by using keyswitches or velocity control.

YouTube is a great resource for learning about a new sampled instrument library. People like Daniel James and Guy Rowland are well known in the industry for doing in-depth overviews and tutorials whenever a new sample library is introduced. If you'd prefer to explore the library on your own time at your own pace, great! Whatever works for you is the right way to do it.

Every company likes to do things their own way when they develop their products. And because no two companies do *everything* the same way, I like to keep a notebook handy with information about things like various instrument groups, and which CC controllers handles various functions such as vibrato or slurring.

Ask yourself some questions about how you will use the library. Is this a product that will become a basic component of your composing style? Perhaps you'll want to integrate the library into your template (*Chapter 8 - The Composing Process*). Maybe even load the entire library onto a slave computer (*Chapter 13 - Recording Your Music*). This library may be an instrument that gets used infrequently and will get loaded into your project on an as-needed basis.

The time you devote now to learning the instrument top-to-bottom will pay off later when you're in the middle of working on a track. Keep those creative right-brain activities separate from the more technical left-brain ones.

Chapter 15 _____

MIXING AND MASTERING

"I don't make music for eyes. I make music for ears." - **Adele**

Broadcast Quality

Is your music "broadcast quality"? Broadcast quality is exactly what it sounds like: good enough to be broadcast on television. What does this mean? Do you need to have your tracks mixed and mastered by a professional to meet this requirement? No. You can achieve this on your own, but it may require education and practice to get your tracks to this level.

Some things to consider:

- Make sure there is no unwanted noise or distortion from your tracks, especially when played at a loud volume. Can you hear a dog barking in the background or a plane flying overhead? Make sure those never get into the track in the first place. If you missed it and can't re-record the track, make sure the mix masks the issue.

- Are the levels of all the instruments consistent and appropriate throughout the piece? If one instrument suddenly gets louder, was there a good reason this happened or was it a mistake?

- Does your music have enough dynamic range? This is the range between the quietest part of your music and the loudest part. It is recommended to have a range of around 8 db.

- Your original recorded tracks should be recorded using 24-bit audio (not 16-bit), even when it will be resampled down to 16-bit audio (most often at 48KHz) as the end product.

WRITING PRODUCTION MUSIC FOR TV

- Is the mix overly compressed? You'll know if your dynamic range is less than the recommended 8 db.

- Does each instrument sit in its own sound space? Are any instruments fighting to be in the same frequency range? When this happens, the mix tends to be muddy. You should be able to distinguish each instrument in the mix.

- Is there too much reverb in the mix? This is easy to hear when played at very low volume. It is likely that your music will sit low in the mix on television so we want to avoid overdoing it with reverb.

- Have you listened to your mix in different listening environments (studio speakers, headphones, car radio, boom box, etc.)? This is a good way to find out if certain instruments stick out in various aural situations. Make sure you listen to your mix using reference monitors with a flat frequency response.

Basic Mixing Plugins

Most DAWs come equipped with basic but essential plugins for mixing *and* mastering:

- **Equalization**

Also known as "EQ", is the process of increasing or decreasing the level (volume) of specific frequencies. A parametric - or multiband - equalizer allows you to pinpoint a series of specific frequencies to change. Each frequency can be widened by expanding the "Q" value. This allows you to affect surrounding frequencies.

- **Compression**

Compressing audio reduces the dynamic range of the music. The quieter parts are increased in volume while the louder parts are lowered in volume. This can give the impression of the entire audio track sounding louder overall.

- **Limiting**

A limiter, like compressors, are dynamics processors. A threshold determines the loudest level - the absolute ceiling - the music can reach.

- **Delay**

A delay effect - also referred to as *echo* - repeats the audio signal. There are two parameters: the amount of time (in milliseconds) between hearing the original and repeated signal; and the number of times the signal repeats. An app for iOS devices, *Tempo Delay Calc*, calculates delay times at specific tempos to match note values (quarter note, eighth note, etc.) and is available at www.hunkydorysoftware.com.

- **Gate**

Also referred to as a *noise gate*, controls the volume of an audio signal. A noise gate silences anything *below* a threshold. This is useful for making sure noisy instruments such as electric guitars are silenced when not playing.

- **Reverb**

Very similar to a delay effect in that sound reflects and echoes for a period of time. The main purpose of reverb is to create a spatial environment by emulating the way different surfaces reflect sound before the sound decays and dissipates. Common reverb types are spring, plate, chamber, digital, and convolution. Convolution technology is the digital sampling of a physical space and applying the properties of that space to your audio signal thereby emulating, for example, a church or even a stairwell.

- **Modulation**

Modulation effects are similar and include Phaser, Chorus, and Flanger effects. Each of these effects use variations of pitch and phase modulation to create sometimes odd and unique sounds.

Additional plugins for advanced usage may also be included with your DAW. In those cases where these types of plugins are *not* included, companies like Waves (www.waves.com) provide plugins covering every possible audio manipulation category:

- **Multiband Compression**

The same as compression, but rather than compressing everything over the entire frequency spectrum, specific frequency ranges (bands) are compressed. This is a useful tool for handling problem areas in your mix.

- **Amplifier Simulation**

Aimed at guitar and bass instruments, amp simulators recreate the sound of a variety of classic amplifiers including distortion and reverb settings. These sounds can be creatively applied to other instruments as well for some unique applications.

- **Saturation**

A distortion effect, saturation originated in the days of analog tape where the audio signal is turned up to a level where the sound "clips". Clipping is normally a bad thing, but can add a certain amount of *edge* to your sound.

- **Distortion**

Distorting an audio signal is usually a bad thing, but this classic effect can be desirable, especially when applied to guitars. It doesn't have to be limited to guitars, though. Being creative with this effect can spark new ideas.

- **Pitch**

Pitch effects not only can correct errant notes but can also transpose notes to another key. There are side-effects of changing the pitch more than a few cents, creating a "chipmunk" effect, which is fine if that's what you're going for. The most famous of these plugins is *Autotune*.

● **Time**

Time effects go hand-in-hand with pitch effects. Notes can be lengthened or shortened. Slowing down a note would cause the pitch to also lower, so that's why you would also apply a pitch effect to correct the difference.

● **Harmonic Enhancement**

Harmonic enhancers provide a limited and specific scope of tonal modifications. There are now many derivations of this tool, but the Aphex Aural Exciter, first introduced in the 1970's, has the *"ability to increase and enhance presence, brightness, and vibrancy on vocal and instrumental tracks alike"*.

● **DeEsser**

Designed for vocals, this tool attenuates sibilance and removes unwanted "essss" (like a snake) and "shhhh" sounds.

● **Noise Reduction and Restoration**

Tools used for cleaning up old recordings remove anomalies such as clicks, pops, hums, crackle, and various undesirable noise.

● **Stereo Imaging**

There is sometimes a need to convert mono sounds into stereo or change the sound to enhance stereo separation and spatial imaging.

● **Surround**

Surround sound mixing is out of the scope of mixing production music for television as music is generally mixed in stereo only. But if you ever have to deliver a mix in 5.1 surround, there are tools available to assist you.

- **Vocal**

Many of the plugins mentioned are designed with vocals in mind. Tools such as the DeEsser, Autotune, Chorus, Aural Exciter, and even Saturation are frequently used with vocal tracks.

How Do You Compare?

Depending on your level of mixing experience, it's always useful to compare your mixes with tracks that have been professionally mixed, or at least have a quality of sound you are striving for. This is called a *reference* track.

It's important to compare apples to apples. If you are creating an orchestral adventure cue then you'll want to compare your work with a similar orchestral action/adventure style cue. Comparing your work to a bluegrass track will be all but useless. To set up a reference track:

- Make sure you're comparing the best quality version of your music. A low-res MP3 will not yield the best results for obvious reasons.

- Use a reference track you know inside and out. Have a good understanding of the instrumentation and structure of the reference track.

- The simplest way is to import the reference track onto a track in your project. Make sure there are no effects (reverb, EQ, etc.) on any bus that would interfere on the reference track's sound.

- Listen with your ears, not your eyes. If you're looking at spectrum analysis tools instead of hearing the music, you're doing yourself a disservice. Match volume by ear. Two things that appear to be the same on a VU meter may not sound the same level. Use your ears!

- Use more than one reference track. No single reference track will be the perfect candidate for our track due to the composition and arrangement. Compare many apples. No bananas, please.

Comparing your mixes to a reference track lets you know whether your cue will be perceived in the same light as the reference tracks you are modeling your mix after. Listen carefully and ask yourself these questions:

- Are the instrument levels balanced? Does anything stick out?

- Is the sound quality too bright? Too dull? Too muddy? Too much low end?

- Is the reverb appropriate for the cue you've written? Are you applying too much or too little?

- How are the instruments panned? Does your mix sound like it could have been recorded in the same room as the reference track?

Switching back and forth between your mix and the reference track's, your goal is for one mix to be indistinguishable from the other.

Hiring Out

When is it necessary to hire a professional to do the job of mixing and/or mastering? Hopefully you'll be able to learn enough as you go to do it all yourself. In the beginning, you may not feel confident enough to do the job. That's okay. You can outright hire someone to do the job for you. You can send your tracks out and they will do the work and send back a finished master.

That's fine, but the big problem with this scenario is that you're not learning anything from it. Try to find someone who can come to *your* studio and work with *your* DAW. Then sit behind them and learn. Ask a lot of questions.

Another option is to trade services. Or as we discussed in *Chapter 10 - Collaboration*, share in revenue from your cue by making the mix engineer a writing partner. Offer them up to 50% of the income from the track's placements. It could end up being very lucrative for the mixer.

It takes time to master (no pun intended) audio mixing. Don't let it hold you back. Do as much as you can on your own. You can't learn unless you try.

> *"Early on I relied on other people for mixing and mastering, but once I learned how to do it myself my productivity went through the roof!"*
> - **Lydia Ashton, composer**

Is Mastering Necessary?

The purpose of mastering is to maintain consistency between seemingly unrelated audio tracks. If you were releasing a CD (or an album under any format) you would want to make sure that each song was at the same approximate volume level. A terrible listener experience would require the listener to turn the volume up and down for every song because the levels are not uniform. The same goes for tonal quality. The EQ should be consistent between all of the tracks.

But what about for production music? If you're creating one track here and there does it still need to be mastered? Probably not. When you mix your track for final release you are already making sure the levels are consistent from start to finish. The same goes for tonal quality - it's consistent all the way through.

Where mastering comes into play is when you are producing a batch of tracks as a project for a client. How is this different from producing songs for an album? It's not. You ensure that every track is consistent in overall volume levels and tonal quality.

Again, do you need to hire out a professional to master your tracks? As with mixing, you can. But the same goals apply here: Learn how to do this on your own. As with the plugins we discussed earlier, many of the tools provided in your DAW already include plugins to be used for mastering: Compression, EQ, and Limiting.

Chapter 16 _____

STEMS AND OTHER DELIVERABLES

"Whenever you find yourself on the side of the majority, it is time to pause and reflect."
- **Mark Twain**

Ship It!

You've reached the finish line. All the hard work of composing, arranging, orchestrating, recording, editing, and mixing your track is complete. You may or may not have a destination for the track(s) you've written. Sometimes you'll be writing tracks in various genres for building up a catalog of potential cues to sell. Other times you'll have a specific client your tracks will be intended for. Let's talk about the latter scenario where you need to deliver your music to a client.

So, what is the client expecting? Two main elements:

- **Stems**
These are the alternate versions of your cues. The number and types of stems will depend on the client's needs.

- **Metadata**
A spreadsheet identifying pertinent information regarding your cues.

Let's talk about what this means.

Stems

The terms "Stems" and "Alternate Mixes" are often used interchangeably in this industry. Stems can be thought of as the individual tracks in your project or even groups of tracks. A flute track can be considered a stem and so can a clarinet track. But the woodwinds group as a whole could also be treated as a stem.

An alternate mix is generally a variation of the main mix by leaving out certain instruments, for example, a mix without any percussion. Technically speaking, a flute stem *could* be considered an alternate mix if the track is interesting enough to stand on its own. For this reason, when we speak of stems we will simplify this nomenclature by referring to *any* of these mixes as "stems".

> *"It's becoming more common for them to ask for actual stems (each instrument part). Some end users don't like a lot of alternate mixes - especially reality shows. I will create stems just to have them available - even if they are not asked for." -* **Matt Hirt, composer**

There is not an industry standard requirement for stems. Stems are alternate versions of your cues. There are *typical* versions you should provide, but it will depend on the music you are writing and the instrumentation in your arrangement.

The primary stem you must include is the *full mix*. This is the cue as you wrote it with all of the instruments playing. The next most used stem is the *no melody* mix. The main reason for this stem is because your melody may interfere with dialogue. This gives editors the option to provide a less obtrusive mix.

> *"Drum 'n Bass is the one stem that I will always grab because it won't compete with dialogue. Drum 'n Bass cues work really well for comedy type cues." -* **Jen Malone, music supervisor**

So what happens if your cue is a solo piano piece? Is it possible to provide a *no melody* mix? There are two ways to approach this: 1) Edit out the melody notes with a MIDI editor (if you're recording a live piano this won't be possible); 2) Re-record a version where you play only an accompaniment - as if you are backing up another instrumentalist playing the melody (such as a flute).

Stems must be able to be lined up in a DAW where each mix starts at the same time. Everything should start as 0:00.00, even if a particular stem contains no sound for several measures! Put yourself in the editor's seat. You would load each stem onto a separate track. Then as the film is playing, the editor can lower the fader of tracks not being used and raise the fader for the track that is needed. That is how the editor can use your *no melody* mix during dialogue and cross-fade back to your *melody mix* when appropriate.

Creating these alternate versions are as simple as muting the tracks (instruments) you do not wish to hear and creating a new mix for the remaining instrument tracks. The following is a list of common and potential types of stems:

- **Full Mix**

This is your primary mix. It contains all of the instruments in the arrangement. This is the version you hope they use because you spent so much time creating it!

- **No Melody**

This is the same as the full mix with the melody instruments muted. This is the mix that gets used more often than not in my experience. The main reason for using this stem is because it won't interfere with dialogue. This mix is also interesting because it will reveal any holes you have in your orchestration when no melody is present. Even without the melody the cue should be interesting and should go *somewhere*.

- **No Drums (percussion)**

This is the same as the full mix with any drum or percussion instrument muted. This does not include melodic percussion instruments such as marimba, vibes, xylophones, or glockenspiel. We are talking about rhythm instruments such as drums (kick, snare, tom toms), shakers, etc.

- **No Melody, No Drums**

Start with the full mix and remove any instruments playing the melody or rhythm. As you can imagine, this is a very sparse mix. This mix has zero chance of interfering with any dialogue.

- **Percussion only**

Just rhythm instruments. It would be rare that this entire stem would be used by itself. It gives the editor a nice option to do a breakdown of the cue. Be careful if you are using any drum loops. If the loop is playing by itself with no additional instrumentation you may violate the *terms of service* of the loop library maker. As a general rule, make sure you read the terms before using any software to know where any potential usage restrictions may apply.

- **Drum and Bass**

This is a common and popular stem. It doesn't apply to every style of music, but it is great to have when possible.

- **Bass only**

Depending on the style of music, a solo bass line: jazz walking bass, funk slap, etc. is similar to the *drums only* mix - it offers a nice option for the editor.

- **No Choir**

For orchestral music, choir libraries that feature "ahs" and "oohs" and quasi-Latin words make a piece sound so much bigger. Removing this instrument really changes the texture of the cue.

- ???

Almost any combination of isolated instruments can be useful if the stem results in an interesting part. Don't get carried away with trying to come up with too many stems. 3 - 6 versions are all you need in most cases.

- **15-, 30-, and 60-second**

These breakdowns are aimed at commercial spots. Not every music library requires these. It can be difficult - depending on the style of music - to create these stems in a way that sounds organic. Consider writing custom versions of your cue to fit these time limits.

- **Stinger**

This one, like the full mix, is a requirement. The stinger is based on the full mix. We've discussed the need for production music cues to end, not fade out. The stinger is the reason why. A stinger is a short version of your cue that leads to this *button* ending. There is no requirement for how long the stinger should be, but - depending on the style of the music and the composition itself - it can be anywhere between 1 to 8 bars long. The stinger stem is the only stem that does *not* have to start where the other stems begin. Editors will place the stinger where it is needed. So, if your cue is 90 seconds long and your stinger is 4 seconds long, you do not have to pad 86 seconds of silence in front of it.

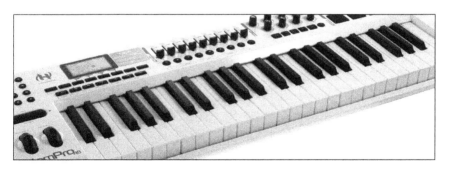

Audio Examples

I have provided audio examples of stems used in television production. The mp3s can be downloaded from https://www.halleonard.com/mylibrary/.

Share the Blame - Dramedy cue
- Track 15 - Share_the_Blame_FULL
- Track 16 - Share_the_Blame_NO_MELODY
- Track 17 - Share_the_Blame_PIZZ_CELESTA
- Track 18 - Share_the_Blame_STINGER

Let's Get Out of Here - Action/Adventure cue
- Track 19 - Let›s Get Out of Here_FULL
- Track 20 - Let›s Get Out of Here_NO SYNTH
- Track 21 - Let›s Get Out of Here_STRINGS ONLY
- Track 22 - Let›s Get Out of Here_STINGER

The Jungle Club - Swing cue
- Track 23 - The_Jungle_Club_FULL
- Track 24 - The_Jungle_Club_NO_MELODY
- Track 25 - The_Jungle_Club_NO_MELODY_NO_PERC
- Track 26 - The_Jungle_Club_PIZZ_ONLY
- Track 27 - The_Jungle_Club_STINGER

Shopping Fever - 50s/60s Pop
- Track 28 - Shopping_Fever_FULL
- Track 29 - Shopping_Fever_NO_MELODY
- Track 30 - Shopping_Fever_NO_MELODY_NO_PERC
- Track 31 - Shopping_Fever_PIZZ_ONLY
- Track 32 - Shopping_Fever_STINGER

Dark Justice - Movie Trailer
- Track 33 - DarkJustice_FULL
- Track 34 - DarkJustice_NOMELODY
- Track 35 - DarkJustice_NOCHOIR
- Track 36 - DarkJustice_STINGER

"Having the longer versions gives you the opportunity to have the track placed in other than commercials and promos. We do a lot of work with corporate where a fair amount of the track will be used."
- ***Edwina Travis-Chin, APM Music***

Audio Formats

When mixing your stems, your client may accept audio in one of two formats: AIFF or WAV. MP3 is almost never accepted other than for use as a preview track when submitting your cue for acceptance into the library. If you submit an MP3, submit nothing less than 192 kbps. 320 kbps is preferable as the quality is higher (closer to CD quality).

Audio for video runs at a sample rate of 48k (khz). If you submit at 44.1k (CD sampling rate), your tracks may be rejected. I have experienced libraries requesting 44.1k audio. I don't know why they ask for this. Probably because they don't know what they're doing. When imported into a video it will have to be resampled to 48k and you risk introducing artifacts into the sound.

Also, even though you are recording your source at 24-bit, mix your stems as 16-bit since this is the industry standard. The audio quality will be higher than if your source was recorded at 16-bit and mixed to 16-bit.

"We have a very specific format we use for trailers, so they tend to sit in a very narrow window between 2 1/2 and 3 1/2 minutes. For musical underscore, such as music for reality projects, will go a bit longer. Rarely does anything go past 3 1/2 to 4 minutes."
- Jeff Rona, Liquid Cinema

Metadata

Metadata is extremely important. It can make or break your chances of getting placements. Unless a library has requested custom music from you, your cues will sit in a catalog to be searched for by potential clients. Those searches will succeed based on the strength of your keywords.

*"We don't want people to over-tag. Saying "this will work for everything" doesn't work. It may be wishful thinking on their part. When you over-tag you get the reputation of not being reliable on your tagging and people will stop going to your library." - **Edwina Travis-Chin, APM Music***

Metadata is often assembled in a spreadsheet (Excel or similar). Each library defines what must be included, but there are general guidelines what information to include. Some libraries may offer an online form to enter the data as part of uploading your tracks.

A separate line of metadata is required for *each* stem you are delivering. Metadata will include the following data:

● **Track Title**

This is the name of the cue, not necessarily the name of the audio file. The library will instruct you on the naming conventions they use for that, if any. We discussed in *Chapter 5 - What is a Cue?*, the importance of cue naming. A name that represents what the cue means emotionally is important from the music supervisor's and/or editor's perspective. A cue named "Untitled (version 3)" says nothing about this music. The wrong name can put obstacles in your way.

- **Stem Version**

This is the identifier that specifies which version this is: full mix, no melody, stinger, etc. The library may have requirements how you name this: full_mix, or Full Mix, or FullMix, or simply FULL.

- **Length**

Indicate the length in minutes and seconds in this format: 1:32. Each stem for a cue should be the same length except for the stinger. The stinger is often just a few seconds long: 0:07.

- **BPM**

A simple designation of the beats-per-minute: 120. The BPM should be the same for every stem.

- **Instrumentation**

Each stem will vary in the instrumentation used. If your full mix contains guitar, bass, piano, drums, and saxophone (melody instrument), your *No Melody* mix would list only guitar, bass, piano, and drums (since the melody instrument, the sax, is not included in this stem).

- **Description**

This is one of the metadata fields you get to take advantage of to help your cue turn up more often in searches. The description should not only describe how the cue can be used, but also the emotion it evokes. For example, *"A warm, heartfelt track with a sense of nostalgia, featuring acoustic piano"*.

- **Genre**

Select a primary genre (see *Appendix A: Music Genres*), such as Country, or Rock, or Hip Hop.

- **Sub-Genre (style)**

The sub-genre, also known as a *style*, can also be selected from *Appendix A: Music Genres*, for example Bluegrass, or Punk Rock.

- **Mood**

The mood describes the emotion that the cue evokes. More than one mood can be selected (see *Appendix B: Moods*). For example, *carefree, confident, happy, joyful,* etc.

- **Keywords**

The keywords are any other descriptive adjectives that can help identify what the cue might be used for. You may sometimes (depending on the library) mention sound-alike artists such as *Rolling Stones*, or *Beyonce*, or *Hans Zimmer*, anything that helps the client identify the type of track this is. Be careful not to over-tag (otherwise known as *metadata spamming*). This might get you search hits, but if it's not anywhere near what the client was expecting it will backfire on you and get you in hot water with the library.

- **Composer(s)**

This is where you will list the name(s) of every composer involved in writing the cue. You will include your name, your PRO affiliation, and your split. For example: Steve Barden ASCAP (50%); Joe Smith BMI (50%).

"Metadata is complex and very demanding. It's one of the most important aspects of our production, right up there with arrangements, mastering, and cut-downs. We have extremely explicit directives from each of our distributors in terms of metadata. So we follow their guidelines, but we do it all here ourselves. We've learned very carefully how to not over tag or under tag any given track. But we always do it to the exact specifications of our distributors as each search engine has different requirements."
- **Jeff Rona, Liquid Cinema**

Chapter 17 _____

BACKING UP YOUR TRACKS

"A satisfied customer is the best business strategy of all." - **Michael LeBoeuf**

Why Backup?

You only need to lose your data once before you realize you need a backup strategy. In my case, it happened twice before I got it in my head I needed to do something about it. That was a hard lesson to learn.

It seems obvious for the need to backup your data, but doing it is another story. There are many ways to backup your projects and some are better than others. But just in case it's not obvious, here are some very important reasons you want to backup your data:

- Your hard drive has crashed with all your projects.

- Your hard drive has filled to capacity and you want to remove older projects to make room for new projects.

- You need to access an older project which is not available on your hard drive.

- Your house has been robbed and your computer was stolen.

- Your house has burned down and you've lost everything (worst-case scenario).

Hopefully your house won't be robbed or burn down, but these are actual scenarios you need to be prepared for. You can always replace lost or stolen equipment, but if your data goes with it, you're done. Let's talk about various ways to backup your data.

Backup Strategies

Many digital formats for backing up data have been available over the years and no doubt newer formats will be available tomorrow. From cassette tapes, to floppy discs, to hard drives, to DAT tapes, to Zip Drives, to CDs, to Blu-ray...it seems like data formats change every few years.

If you have backed up your data to any of these formats, what happens when a newer format is introduced, or the format you've used is now obsolete (like Zip Drives)? Should you transfer all of your work from the old format to a newer one? That seems like an awful lot of work, especially as the amount of your data grows over the years.

It would be wonderful if the format you choose is guaranteed to be around forever. Unfortunately, that will never be the case. Even formats like hard drives and CDs that have outlasted many other formats will one day be obsolete.

No matter what format you choose, if you don't store your backup offsite you're at risk. Offsite means anywhere that is not where your studio computer is. This could be a storage facility, your mom's house, or even a friend's home or office. Storing the backups in your garage is not the same as *offsite*. In the worst-case scenario of your house burning down, if those backups are still on the premises then you may as well not have backed up at all.

An alternate method for backing up data to physical media is *cloud backup*. The "cloud" is not some magical place in the sky. Think of it as someone else's computer and you don't know where that computer lives. Services such as Carbonite (www.carbonite.com), Box (www.box.com), and DropBox (www.dropbox.com) are Internet-based backup/storage services. I personally use Carbonite. It runs in the background and backs up your computer as data changes.

I consider cloud backup as a last resort safety measure. I encourage you to also have redundant backups locally for convenience. Storing backups on a secondary hard drive (such as an external drive) is a quick way to have your data available should the need arise. Having your data in only one place is just asking for trouble. Having your data in two places is better than nothing. Having your data in three places is strongly encouraged.

> *"A file doesn't really exist until it can be found on multiple drives."*
> **- Lydia Ashton, composer**

Points to remember:

- Backup often

- Backup everyday

- Backup right now

- Don't forget to backup!

- Have you backed up yet?

Rendering MIDI to Audio

As I mentioned in *Chapter 13 - Recording Your Music*, there is a need to create backups of *individual MIDI tracks*. Why is this important? There will be a time when you need to open an older project. It may be to remix the cue for a new client, or create an alternate mix (stem) such as a 30-second version you didn't provide.

You may discover that one or more of your MIDI tracks were using a sample library you no longer have available. This would be the case for those subscription sample libraries you were "renting".

Another scenario is that you update your sample libraries every year or so to improve the sounds with newer and better sounding samples. This could make it impossible to simply *drop in* the newer library because the keyswitches may be different, or the articulations are handled differently, or any number of differences making your MIDI tracks next to useless.

The solution is to render your MIDI tracks to audio. Consider this as a *sub-backup*. Most DAWs provide a way to select each track and mix it down to a separate audio track. I would recommend mixing each of these tracks *within* your project (as opposed to creating external WAV or AIFF files). Think of each track as another stem. So now, even if those older sample libraries are gone, you can at least remix the cue with the original sounds intact. Problem solved!

Later, you will backup this project using one of the above-mentioned backup strategies and each rendered MIDI track will be backed up along with it! If you've not done this for those projects, it might be a good idea to do this now - before those sample libraries get replaced.

Chapter 18 _____

ORGANIZING YOUR LIFE

"Chaos is not a strategy." - **Author**

Personality Types

Some people seem to be born with inordinate organizational skills. We all knew someone like that in high school or college. Others seem to muddle through life barely keeping it together. Regardless of the whether you fall in with Team Organized or Team Chaos, you will have to become mentally disciplined if you want to succeed in this business.

The personality types of organized and disorganized persons can be summarized by these general traits:

Organized
- Follows a regimented schedule. If something's not on a to-do list it doesn't get done
- Always on-time for appointments
- Your life is clutter-free. Everything has a place and you will find it there when it's not being used
- You are optimistic. You have a "can-do" attitude

Disorganized
- The idea of "getting organized" sets you in a mental tailspin
- Feeling easily overwhelmed
- Unable to meet deadlines and keep commitments
- Never puts things away and can't locate things later when needed
- Never gets rid of things (hoarder)

Why This Is Important

Some of us are extremely organized and while others are the exact opposite. Looking at the list above you probably recognize traits from both categories in yourself. Does this affect how creative we are? No. Those living in total chaos can be just as creative as those who aren't.

Being organized makes you more efficient. It allows you to do the things you do best. Composing music comprises both left- and right-brain activities. The analytical side (left) and the creative side (right) are both important brain functions, but when you're deep in the composing process the worst thing that can happen is a disruption of your right-brain creative flow because you're hunting for that perfect sound in your DAW. This can lead you down a rabbit hole and ruin your compositional train of thought.

This type of distraction should be called the *YouTube Syndrome*. I'm pretty sure I just made that up. If you've ever spent any amount of time perusing YouTube you know how easy it is to look for a specific video and explore the many "recommendations". Before you know it, you've spent several hours watching too many videos having nothing to do with your original goal.

> *"I have a spreadsheet that serves as my rolodex. I keep info on name, address/phone/email, how we learned to know each other, what they work with (composer, copyist, producer, etc), when we spoke last, and what that contact was about." -* **Lydia Ashton, composer**

Anybody can learn how to be organized. Here are suggestions to get you going:

- **Write everything down (computer or paper)**
It clears your mind so you can remain more creative. You don't *have to* remember it because it's written down. But it *can* help you remember things just by doing it. The physical act of writing on paper (not the computer) triggers a mental association with the thing you've written.

- **Declutter your work area**

Your work area should be minimalistic. You only need the things you need at any given moment. The more clutter you have, the more you are inviting more clutter.

- **Put things away when you're finished with them**

This is part of decluttering. As soon as you are finished with something, put it away. It keeps your work area clear and you will always know where it is when you need it again. The more clutter you have the harder it will be to find things.

- **Group tasks into similar functions**
  (see also *Chapter 12 - Managing Your Time*)

Make all your phone calls at one time. Answer your emails at one time. Jumping back and forth creates chaos and makes it easier to forget what you were doing. Your tasks are defined by a schedule. Stick to it.

- **Create action plans and set priorities**

An action plan is not the same as a schedule. It's the first step of creating one. The action plan is a list of things you want or need to accomplish on any day. Once you have your items, prioritize them. Set reasonable expectations for completing the tasks.

- **Distinguish between important tasks and trivial ones**

Not every task is important, yet it still needs to be done. Emptying your waste basket is not a critical task, but it still needs to be done at some point. Prioritize accordingly.

- **Create a daily schedule**

Your schedule is your list of tasks for each day and each week. Set time limits for each task. Be flexible with the time. Things come up and you have to be relaxed about it.

- **Set alarms and reminders**

Alarms and reminders are not just useful for appointments. Setting limits on how much time you spend on email might need an alarm to remind you to move on to the next task. Most smartphones have calendars built in with alarms and timers, and they're always with you!

- **Delegate**

Ask for help when you can't do it all by yourself. Delegate tasks to others if possible. Even for the small things like emptying your waste basket. If you have kids, have them help out. Make them part of the team, they want to be part of your life.

- **Stay focused**

Force yourself to stay focused and work hard. Remove any distractions around you. Turn off the TV unless you're using it for research. Stay off social media. This will drag you down a rabbit hole. If you have chores to do, get them done before starting your music work.

- **Eat well and exercise**

Stay away from junk food. Too many calories with little nutritional value. Sleep is also extremely important. You will be more creative if you are well rested. Exercise helps relieve stress. Take care of your physical and mental state at all costs. Get up and move around. Don't stay seated for too long without breaks.

- **Think positive!**

Stay away from negative thoughts. Focus your energy on the joy of creating music. Remind yourself you are on a journey. The destination is not getting your music on this one TV show or getting into this one music library. The destination is here and now. You've reached it. You're doing it.

- **Me Time**

Allow for some "me time" at the end of the day. All work and no play is not only detrimental to your state of mind, but it can have adverse effects to those around you. You deserve to relax and have fun.

Organization Software

Pencil and paper is all you need to make a schedule. A daily planner is what we used before computers. That technology still works. But if you insist on being high tech, there are many software solutions available to you.

Much of the software needed is already available on your smartphone. Others can be downloaded for little or no cost. The various programs (or apps if you're doing everything on your smartphone or tablet) can be broken down into the following categories:

- **Time Tracking**

Time tracking is useful if you're working on a project for a client and you are billing by the hour. Time tracking functionality is often part of bookkeeping software such as *Quickbooks* for when you will send an invoice to a client.

- **Scheduler / Calendar**

We've all had monthly paper calendars with cute cat pictures hanging in our office or from the refrigerator for years. We write important events on a day specifying the time to be somewhere. The same concept is available on your computer and smartphones - maybe without the cute cat pictures. Reminders and alarms can be set as well as setting up recurring events. *Google Calendar* is a cloud-based application that can be accessed anywhere you have Internet access. It also includes *Google Tasks*.

● Contacts

Also known as an *address book*, a contacts list organizes your list of family, friends, business associates, clients, etc. containing their name, phone number, mailing address, email, and many custom fields such as birthday (important to acknowledge!), names of kids, food allergies, and any other information that makes your business relationship more personal. It may also link with calendar software for setting up reminders of appointments and important dates.

● To-Do Lists / Task Management

The most common of organizational software, the basic functionality lets you define a list of things "to do", order them by priority, then check them off when they have been completed. More advanced software can help you break down a big task into smaller, more manageable chunks.

● Spreadsheet

Microsoft Excel is the most commonly used spreadsheet on both Windows and Mac computers, but Google Docs provides free spreadsheet cloud-based software that contains the most commonly used features of Excel. The best reason for using a spreadsheet is that it is customizable to you. Commercial software for tracking things like expenses and mileage may not do everything you need so why not start with a spreadsheet until you find the right software for you?

- **Expenses / Receipts**

Anything that is tax deductible you will want to keep track of. This includes musical gear, sound libraries, software, gas, food, lodging, airlines, etc. If these are deductions keep accurate records in case you get audited later on, which could be up to 3 years (Federal regulations) from the time you file your tax return.

- **Mileage**

You can always jot an entry in a notebook or a post-it note or enter your mileage in a spreadsheet. Mileage is a great tax deduction. Any time you make a trip for business you'll want to keep track of mileage. There are now apps that use GPS to calculate your mileage automatically. The only thing you need to remember to do is start the app.

- **Music cue database**

This software is specific to the music production industry. You'll want to keep track of every cue you write. Not only will you keep track of things like which music library the cue is in, but it also helps when naming a cue ("Did I already write a cue called *Nobody Home?*").

You can create a spreadsheet that contains the fields you need, or use generic database software such as Microsoft Access or Filemaker Pro. Whatever you use you want to make sure the data is searchable.

I will mention a product called *Composer Catalog* (www. composercatalog.com). This software is unique for this industry. There aren't a lot of alternatives. Full disclosure: This software is written by a colleague of mine, Keith LuBrant. A talented musician and composer in his own right. I'm happy to support his efforts. This is a superb product.

The Composer Catalog software stores all of the information you'll need about your cues, including:

- Cue info: name, genre, key, tempo, BPM, PRO registration date
- Writer's information includes PRO affiliation and splits
- Publisher's info
- Ability to play the cue from the software
- Built in reminders for sending contracts, filing taxes, etc.
- All of the metadata you would ever need to include
- List of session musicians used in recording
- Graphical statistic of publishers, genres
- Many, many other great features

Take advantage of all the great software out there to help you keep organized and on-track. Spend more time composing music instead of figuring out where the extra staples are.

Part 4

Money Matters

WRITING PRODUCTION MUSIC FOR TV

Chapter 19 _____

HOW MUCH MONEY CAN YOU MAKE?

"You need to assign some sort of value to what you're doing in order for your product to be valued." - **Edwina Travis-Chin**

The Value of Placements

There are two ways to earn money from placing your music in television: License fees and royalties. License fees, in the form of a sync license, vary widely. Of course, when a sync license is available. Not all music libraries feel the need to split the license with you. Part of the reason for this is when a blanket license covers dozens or hundreds of tracks being delivered to a client. In that case, it becomes a bookkeeping nightmare to figure the splits for every composer included in the deliverable.

When libraries split the license with you, expect a 50/50 split. This is common, but not guaranteed. If you are fortunate enough to bypass the middleman, i.e. the library, and place it yourself the entire sync license fee is all yours. How much can you make on a sync license? If you're placing a vocal song through an ad agency for a commercial or placing a song in a major film, a sync fee can reach upwards of $100,000 or more. These types of placements are not as frequent as music for television. There are more hours of broadcasting to fill than there are for commercials and films. These are the placements you will see most of.

Because of the need for bulk music tracks, the fees available will be considerably smaller. Fees follow the supply-and-demand business model. Since there are many suppliers of music all vying for the same opportunities it makes sense that the fees will be minimal. These fees can range anywhere from $1 up to a few hundred dollars.

The second way you'll earn money is from performance royalties. As you'll learn in the next chapter (*Chapter 20 - Performance Rights Organizations*), PROs pay out royalties based on many factors for the

performance of your music in television. Let's look at some actual royalty statements and see how much money is paid.

> *"I find that some composers do it as a way to make money but don't really enjoy it. If you like it and it's fulfilling for you then dedicate yourself to it. Understand that it takes a long time to get somewhere because it's a slow-moving field and you won't make a lot of money quickly."*
> *- Matt Hirt, composer*

Royalty Statements

In a nutshell, PROs collect license fees from broadcasters (ABC, CBS, FOX, NBC, and cable networks). These collected fees are used to pay composers and publishers their fair share depending on the usage. For example, time of day factors into calculating the dollar amount. ASCAP (my PRO affiliation) breaks it down like this:

- Morning (7:00am – 12:59pm) 50%
- Afternoon (1:00pm – 6:59pm) 75%
- Primetime (7:00pm – 12:59am) 100%
- Night (1:00am – 6:59am) 25%

As you can see, shows that are broadcast in Primetime (7 pm to 1 am) pay the full amount because that's when most people are watching television. The lowest rated time is Night (1 am to 7 am). Most people are asleep during those hours so the audience is smaller.

Figure 19-1 below, is a page from an actual ASCAP Domestic Writers royalty statement. The data included here contains the series name, the episode name, the title of the cue as it is registered by the publisher with the PRO, the day part (M, A, P, N, as described above), the number of times the cues was played, the performance type, its duration, total number of credits earned, and the dollar royalty amount.

Figure 19-1

Line #	Series / Film	Episode Name or Date	Title	Work ID	CA %	Share %	Service Name	C/S	Day Part	# of Plays	Perf. Type	Duration HH:MM:SS	Total Credits	Royalty Amount
000076	LEAH REMINI: ITS ALL RELATIVE	PUTTING THE FUN IN FUNERAL	GURNEY SONG_33198 KKF3_RED RICMA	00887472943	100.00%	25.00%	TLC	C	P	6	BG	00:00:21	1.85538	$13.91538
000077	LEAH REMINI: ITS ALL RELATIVE	THE BREAST BIRTHDAY EVER	GURNEY SONG_38742 KKF4_RED RICMA	00887475208	100.00%	50.00%	TLC	C	N	1	BG	00:00:27	0.19873	$1.49044
000078	LEAH REMINI: ITS ALL RELATIVE	THE BREAST BIRTHDAY EVER	GURNEY SONG_38742 KKF4_RED RICMA	00887475208	100.00%	50.00%	TLC	C	P	4	BG	00:00:27	3.17964	$23.84716
000079	LEAH REMINI: ITS ALL RELATIVE	THE BREAST BIRTHDAY EVER	GURNEY SONG_46344 KKF4_RED RICMA	00887491754	100.00%	25.00%	TLC	C	N	1	BG	00:00:37	0.13640	$1.02298
000080	LEAH REMINI: ITS ALL RELATIVE	THE BREAST BIRTHDAY EVER	GURNEY SONG_46344 KKF4_RED RICMA	00887491754	100.00%	25.00%	TLC	C	P	4	BG	00:00:37	2.17996	$16.34980
000081	LEAH REMINI: ITS ALL RELATIVE	WELCOME TO THE FAMILY	GURNEY SONG_33198 KKF3_RED RICMA	00887472943	100.00%	25.00%	TLC	C	N	1	BG	00:00:29	0.10689	$0.80168
000082	LEAH REMINI: ITS ALL RELATIVE	WELCOME TO THE FAMILY	GURNEY SONG_33198 KKF3_RED RICMA	00887472943	100.00%	25.00%	TLC	C	P	6	BG	00:00:29	2.56176	$19.21320
000083	LITTLE COUPLE	JENS BIG 4-0	LITTLE COUPLE CUES	00884140904	100.00%	25.00%	TLC	C	N	1	BG	00:00:20	0.07347	$0.55101
000084	LITTLE COUPLE	JENS BIG 4-0	LITTLE COUPLE CUES	00884140904	100.00%	25.00%	TLC	C	P	5	BG	00:00:20	1.47240	$11.04280
000085	NIGHTMARE CHRISTMAS	2014-07-26	KKF3 FILLER INSTINCT A	00883627268	100.00%	25.00%	DINV	C	N	1	BG	00:00:40	0.04848	$0.36358
000086	NIGHTMARE CHRISTMAS	2014-07-26	KKF4 MIDNIGHT SNATCH A	00883628541	100.00%	50.00%	DINV	C	N	1	BG	00:00:29	0.07046	$0.52841
000087	NIGHTMARE CHRISTMAS	2014-07-26	KKL HOLIDAY WISHES 1A	00884063816	100.00%	25.00%	DINV	C	N	1	BG	00:00:36	0.04338	$0.32518
000088	SERIOUSLY FUNNY KIDS	KLUMOSAURUS REX	SERIOUSLY FUNNY KIDS CUES	00883282160	100.00%	25.00%	LRW	C	A	2	BG	00:00:30	0.00542	$0.04062
000089	SERIOUSLY FUNNY KIDS	THE DIFFERENCE BETWEEN BOYS AND GIRLS	SERIOUSLY FUNNY KIDS CUES	00883282160	100.00%	25.00%	LRW	C	A	3	BG	00:00:54	0.01266	$0.09483
000090	SNOOKI AND JWOWW	COUPLES WEEKEND	WATCHING FOR SIGNS	00884592211	100.00%	50.00%	MTV3	C	P	8	BG	00:00:56	0.72352	$5.42576
000091	SNOOKI AND JWOWW	LET THE PLANNING BEGIN	FIVE KISSES	00884590885	100.00%	50.00%	MTV3	C	P	1	BG	00:00:43	0.06922	$0.51915

Credits is a designation that ASCAP uses to determine the value of the placement. The formula for calculating the credit is rather complicated, but if you're interested this is how they do it:

Use Weight x Licensee Weight x "Follow the Dollar" Factor x Time of Day Weight + Premium Credits = Total Credits

For a detailed explanation of this formula, visit the ASCAP website:

https://www.ascap.com/help/royalties-and-payment/payment/royalties

For the sake of comparison, we'll look at similar royalty statements for BMI. Figure 19-2 shows a Domestic Writers royalties statement:

U.S. Performances - Cable Television

Source											
Series/Film		Episode	Work Number	Performance			Your %	WH	Current Activity	Super Usage	Royalty Amt
Count	Title			Use	Timing	Period					
LIFETIME											
	PREACHERS DAUGHTERS	JUDGMENT DAY									
2	ON THE BRINK		011382327	BI	00:48	20152	50.00%		$12.68	$0.00	$12.#
	LIFETIME Total										$15.8
LIFETIME MOVIE											
	MURDER IN MEXICO										
2	BRAZIL I KNOW		020882554	SVI	01:15	20181	50.00%		$12.81	$6.41	$19.2
2	MURDER IN MEXICO-CUES		000000000	BI	00:55	20181	50.00%		$4.11	$0.00	$4.1
	LIFETIME MOVIE Total										$23.3
LIFETIME WOMEN											
	PREACHERS DAUGHTERS	JUDGMENT DAY									
2	ON THE BRINK		011382327	BI	00:48	20152	50.00%		$0.11	$0.00	$0.#
	ROSEANNE S NUTS	MOTHER S DAY									
10	DANCE OF LOVE		011874987	BI	00:22	20181	50.00%		$0.18	$0.00	$0.:
	LIFETIME WOMEN Total										$0.2
LOGO											
	A LIST NEW YORK	EPISODE 204									
1	BEACHCOMBIN JP		013486402	BI	00:30	20181	50.00%		$0.26	$0.00	$0.2
	LOGO Total										$0.2#
MSG											
	BEGINNINGS	JOHN MOORE									
2	SIMPLY FUN JP		013486456	BI	00:31	20181	50.00%		$4.46	$0.00	$4.4
	MSG Total										$4.46
MSG PLUS											
	ULTIMATE FIGHTING CHAMPIONSHIP	UFC 144 MAIN EVENT									
3	HIT THE GROUND RUNNING JP		013789827	BI	00:41	20181	50.00%		$4.32	$0.00	$4.3.
3	JUMP THE GUN JP		013789673	BI	00:46	20181	50.00%		$4.84	$0.00	$4.8#
	MSG PLUS Total										$9.18

Figure 19-2

In the ASCAP statement example, you may have noticed that all of these shows aired on cable networks (TLC, Investigation Discovery, Lifetime, and MTV). The royalty amounts are lower than the major networks (ABC, CBS, FOX, and NBC). For BMI, the statement covers shows on Lifetime, Logo, and MSG Networks.

In contrast, let's take a look at royalties paid from broadcasts on streaming services. Figure 19-3 below lists ASCAP placements from shows broadcast on HULU. Notice that the number of plays is in the tens of thousands, and yet the royalty payment appears small compared to cable broadcasting. Each play on a streaming service may only account for one or two people watching the episode, whereas a play on a cable network represents thousand or even millions of viewers for that episode. While it looks like the streaming numbers are unfairly weighted, in actuality, they are comparable. As streaming services mature it is likely that these

ternet: Audio/Visual - HULU

Line #	Series / Film	Episode Name or Date	Title	Work ID	CA %	Share %	C/S	# of Plays	Perf. Type	Duration HH:MM:SS	Premium Credits	Credits	Royalty Amount
001	KEEPING UP WITH THE KARDASHIANS	2 BIRTHDAYS AND A YARD SALE	A STORM IS BREWING	00884591432	100.00%	50.00%	C	103,832	BG	00:00:18	0.00000	0.07302	$0.60972
002	KEEPING UP WITH THE KARDASHIANS	A VERY MERRY CHRISTMAS	SIDEKICK MISCHIEF	00885636320	100.00%	50.00%	C	76,400	BG	00:00:52	0.00000	0.15520	$1.29592
003	KEEPING UP WITH THE KARDASHIANS	BACKDOOR BRUISER	CHALLENGE ACCEPTED	00884592490	100.00%	50.00%	C	72,768	BG	00:00:19	0.00000	0.05401	$0.45096
004	KEEPING UP WITH THE KARDASHIANS	COLOR ME LONELY	CHALLENGE ACCEPTED	00884592490	100.00%	50.00%	C	85,875	BG	00:00:13	0.00000	0.04361	$0.36414
005	KEEPING UP WITH THE KARDASHIANS	GREECE HIM UP	CHALLENGE ACCEPTED	00884592490	100.00%	50.00%	C	81,518	BG	00:00:19	0.00000	0.06051	$0.50526
006	KEEPING UP WITH THE KARDASHIANS	HOME IS WHERE YOUR MOM IS	EAVESDROPPING	00884590884	100.00%	50.00%	C	82,391	BG	00:00:31	0.00000	0.09978	$0.83316
007	KEEPING UP WITH THE KARDASHIANS	HOW TO DEAL	GUILT BY ASSOCIATION	00885636236	100.00%	50.00%	C	104,300	BG	00:00:23	0.00000	0.09372	$0.78256
008	KEEPING UP WITH THE KARDASHIANS	KYLIE S SWEET 16	PANTHER LIKE	00884591035	100.00%	50.00%	C	81,783	BG	00:00:42	0.00000	0.13419	$1.12049
009	KEEPING UP WITH THE KARDASHIANS	LIFE S A BEACH HOUSE	EAVESDROPPING	00884590884	100.00%	50.00%	C	77,836	BG	00:00:16	0.00000	0.04853	$0.40523
010	KEEPING UP WITH THE KARDASHIANS	PAPARAZZI AND PAPAS	SHARE THE BLAME	00884591186	100.00%	50.00%	C	72,209	BG	00:00:15	0.00000	0.04232	$0.35337
011	KEEPING UP WITH THE KARDASHIANS	ROCKING THE CRADLE 90 MIN	A STORM IS BREWING	00884591432	100.00%	50.00%	C	95,171	BG	00:00:24	0.00000	0.08923	$0.74507
012	KEEPING UP WITH THE KARDASHIANS	SURPRISE ENGAGEMENT PART 1	CHALLENGE ACCEPTED	00884592490	100.00%	50.00%	C	103,807	BG	00:00:20	0.00000	0.08111	$0.67727
013	LITTLE COUPLE	WELCOME HOME, WILLI	KKF3 LIKE SNOW A	00883627681	100.00%	25.00%		51,200	T	00:00:39	0.00000	0.18002	$1.50317
014	LITTLE COUPLE	WELCOME HOME, WILLI	KKF3 LIKE SNOW A	00883627681	100.00%	25.00%		51,200	T	00:00:01	0.00000	0.01800	$0.15030
015	LITTLE COUPLE	WELCOME HOME, WILLI	LITTLE COUPLE CUES	00884140904	100.00%	25.00%		51,200	BG	00:00:12	0.00000	0.01200	$0.10020
016	LITTLE COUPLE	ZOEYS BIRTHDAY PARTY	KKF4 CRAZY CRICKET A	00883626713	100.00%	50.00%	C	42,298	BG	00:00:14	0.00000	0.02314	$0.19322
017	SNOOKI AND JWOWW	301	A STORM IS BREWING	00884591432	100.00%	50.00%	C	57,466	BG	00:00:09	0.00000	0.02021	$0.16875
018	SNOOKI AND JWOWW	301	CLUELESS BASTARD	00884590722	100.00%	50.00%	C	57,466	BG	00:00:09	0.00000	0.02021	$0.16875
019	SNOOKI AND JWOWW	301	PANTHER LIKE	00884591035	100.00%	50.00%	C	57,466	BG	00:00:14	0.00000	0.03143	$0.26244
020	SNOOKI AND JWOWW	301	SIMPLY	00884591187	100.00%	50.00%	C	57,466	BG	00:00:05	0.00000	0.01123	$0.09377
021	SNOOKI AND JWOWW	COUPLES WEEKEND	WATCHING FOR SIGNS	00884592211	100.00%	50.00%	C	47,266	BG	00:00:56	0.00000	0.10348	$0.86406

Figure 19-3

numbers will increase.

Figure 19-4 shows a similar statement covering HULU broadcasts for BMI:

U.S. Performances - Internet Audiovisual

Source										
Series/Film		Episode	Work	Performance			Your %	WH	Current	Super Usage	Royalty Amt
Count	Title		Number	Use	Timing	Period			Activity		
HULU											
LONG ISLAND MEDIUM		CHINESE NEW YEAR									
19,300	FUN WITH CHOPSTICKS JP		013486664	BI	00:30	20161	50.00%		$0.10	$0.00	$0.1
LONG ISLAND MEDIUM		CHRISTMAS SPECIAL									
29,616	DECK THE HALLS HIP HOP V1 JP		013789378	BI	00:14	20161	50.00%		$0.07	$0.00	$0.0
29,616	O CHRISTMAS TREE V5 JP		013789449	BI	00:36	20161	50.00%		$0.19	$0.00	$0.1
LUCKY DOG		ROSIE									
2,822	LUCKY DOG-CUES		000000000	BI	00:46	20161	25.00%		$0.01	$0.00	$0.0
MILLIONAIRE MATCHMAKER		ALPHA FEMALES									
16,092	ENTI FRAGILE HEARTS		012646862	BI	00:27	20161	50.00%		$0.08	$0.00	$0.0
MILLIONAIRE MATCHMAKER		RETURN OF ROBIN KASSNER									
15,113	ENTI FRAGILE HEARTS		012646862	BI	00:12	20161	50.00%		$0.03	$0.00	$0.0
MOB WIVES		CAUGHT ON TAPE									
48,113	HITTING A NERVE		015939283	BI	00:36	20161	50.00%		$0.30	$0.00	$0.3
48,113	HITTING A NERVE NO STRING MIX		015939288	BI	00:04	20161	50.00%		$0.03	$0.00	$0.0
MOB WIVES		FIGHTS AND FACIALS									
49,175	UNRESOLVED ISSUES		013138747	BI	01:03	20161	50.00%		$0.54	$0.00	$0.5
MOB WIVES		FIRE AWAY									
43,094	ANXIOUS MOMENTS		013208808	BI	00:29	20161	50.00%		$0.22	$0.00	$0.2
MOB WIVES		MAKE UPS AND BREAK UPS									
56,583	UNRESOLVED ISSUES DRUM AND BAS		013208801	BI	00:25	20161	50.00%		$0.25	$0.00	$0.2
56,583	UNRESOLVED ISSUES UNDERSCORE M		013138750	BI	00:09	20161	50.00%		$0.09	$0.00	$0.0
MOB WIVES		OF VICE AND MEN									
43,554	UNRESOLVED ISSUES		013138747	BI	00:24	20161	50.00%		$0.18	$0.00	$0.1
MOB WIVES		VEGAS PART THREE									
44,234	HITTING A NERVE		015939283	BI	00:28	20161	50.00%		$0.22	$0.00	$0.2
44,234	UNRESOLVED ISSUES NO SYNTH MIX		013138751	BI	00:04	20161	50.00%		$0.03	$0.00	$0.0
44,234	UNRESOLVED ISSUES UNDERSCORE M		013138750	BI	00:19	20161	50.00%		$0.15	$0.00	$0.1

Figure 19-4

Finally, we'll take a look at *International Royalties*. In figure 19-5, this ASCAP example demonstrates the royalties for shows broadcast in Canada. The information is not as detailed as the Domestic royalties statement. Only the series, episode, cue title, and royalty amount is given.

Line #	Title	Program	Episode	Total US Dollars
000001	A STORM IS BREWING	KEEPING UP WITH THE KARDASHIAN	2 BIRTHDAYS AND A YARD SALE	$0.1
000002	BLUE TEARS	EX AND THE WHY	109	$0.1
000003	CHALLENGE ACCEPTED	KEEPING UP WITH THE KARDASHIAN	BACKDOOR BRUISER	$0.8
000004	CHALLENGE ACCEPTED	KEEPING UP WITH THE KARDASHIAN	GREECE HIM UP	$0.6
000005	CHALLENGE ACCEPTED	KEEPING UP WITH THE KARDASHIAN	SURPRISE ENGAGEMENT PART 1	$0.1
000006	DEADLY WIVES CUES	DEADLY WIVES	WHERE THERE S A WILL THERE S A	$0.1
000007	DEADLY WIVES CUES	DEADLY WIVES	CRAVEN FOR MURDER	$0.8
000008	DEADLY WIVES CUES	DEADLY WIVES	LIARS CLUB	$0.4
000009	EAVESDROPPING	KEEPING UP WITH THE KARDASHIAN	HOME IS WHERE YOUR MOM IS	$1.1
000010	EAVESDROPPING	KEEPING UP WITH THE KARDASHIAN	LIFE S A BEACH HOUSE	$0.6
000011	FEAR THE DARK	DOOMSDAY PREPPERS	INTO THE SPIDER HOLE	$0.9
000012	GUILT BY ASSOCIATION	KEEPING UP WITH THE KARDASHIAN	HOW TO DEAL	$0.1
000013	KKF3 ANIMATED TOYS A	LITTLE COUPLE	BACK TO WORK	$0.3
000014	KKF3 ANIMATED TOYS A	LITTLE COUPLE	COUNTDOWN TO INDIA	$1.5
000015	KKF3 ANIMATED TOYS A	LITTLE COUPLE	CHECK UP TIME	$0.2
000016	KKF3 ANIMATED TOYS A	SAND MASTERS	HAWAII	$0.25
000017	KKF3 BANANA JELLO A	LITTLE COUPLE	ALL YOU WANTED TO KNOW	$1.08
000018	KKF3 BANANA JELLO A	LITTLE COUPLE	MAKING A SPLASH	$0.4
000019	KKF3 BANANA JELLO A	LITTLE COUPLE	AND HIS NAME IS	$0.2
000020	KKF3 BANANA JELLO A	NOVA	RISE OF THE ROBOTS	$0.25
000021	KKF3 FILLER INSTINCT A	EAT THE STORY OF FOOD	HOOKED ON SEAFOOD	$1.84
000022	KKF3 FLIP HER WIG A	LITTLE COUPLE	CHECK UP TIME	$0.3
000023	KKF3 LIKE SNOW A	LITTLE COUPLE	FOUR LITTLE EMBRYOS	$0.73
000024	KKF3 LIKE SNOW A	LITTLE COUPLE	AND HIS NAME IS	$0.6
000025	KKF3 LIKE SNOW A	LITTLE COUPLE	WELCOME HOME WILL	$0.83
000026	KKF3 LIKE SNOW A	LITTLE COUPLE	BACK TO BUSINESS	$1.68
000027	KKF3 LIMBO SHOPPING A	SAND MASTERS	ASPEN	$0.27
000028	KKF3 MOLDY BREAD A	SAND MASTERS	HAWAII	$0.28

Figure 19-5

WRITING PRODUCTION MUSIC FOR TV

As you can see, the dollar amounts for each placement are not large. In fact, a single placement *might* buy you a cup of coffee at Starbucks. That's why it's important to get as much music out there that you can. It truly is a *numbers* game.

Figure 19-6 shows a similar statement covering International broadcasts for BMI, also for Canada:

ternational Performances - Audiovisual

Country / Society								
Series / Film		Episode						
Title			Work Number	Performance		Adj	WH	Royalty Amt
				Source	Period			
ANADA - SOCAN								
TABLOID		EASY MONEY						
	HIDDEN DANGER		000000000	TELEVISION				$0.50
	HITTING A NERVE		000000000	TELEVISION				$0.18
TODDLERS AND TIARAS SERIES		BEAUTIFUL ME 50 S PAGEANT						
	TODDLERS AND TIARAS SERIES		000000000	TELEVISION				$0.23
TRUE LIFE		I M SAVING DETROIT						
	COSMIC BREEZE		000000000	TELEVISION				$0.13
UNLIKELY ANIMAL FRIENDS								
	JOCA FRIED POSSUM		000000000	FILM				$0.15
WHAT NOT TO WEAR		NOEL						
	DIXIE STRUT JP		000000000	TELEVISION				$0.75
1 GIRL 5 GAYS								
	BRIGHT SPOT JP		000000000	FILM				$0.01
	PUKA SHELLS JP		000000000	FILM				$0.18
	SIMPLY FUN JP		000000000	FILM				$0.03

gure 19-6

Tracking Your Placements

So how do you know when your music is placed on a show? Better yet, how do you know when it airs? The music library that made the placement on your behalf *may* let you know when your cue has been placed. But more often than not, you will not be notified. Depending how busy the library is, they may not have the resources to contact every composer when something good happens. If it's a significant placement then they will want to share the good news with you.

Unless you are watching the show and hear your music, you may not know about the placement until the cue sheet is filed with your PRO. It's always exciting to see another new TV show that has selected your music. I once experienced hearing my music by accident. I was doing something and the TV was on in the background. I think my wife was watching one of those cooking shows. I heard one of my cues and my ears immediately perked up! Even if the music is mixed low in the background under dialogue, you'll *know* if it's your music.

Another way to know when your music has been used in a show is by using a service such as Tunesat (www.tunesat.com). Tunesat will "fingerprint" your music (more on this below). Their service will monitor every TV show that is being broadcast and detect when your music is being played during the show by matching it with the fingerprint. It's quite an amazing technology. It will listen to the audio being played and extract any music - even if it is under dialogue - and run their algorithm using *digital pattern recognition* to see if it matches any music (hopefully yours) in their database.

I use this service and can attest to its success. Occasionally they will report a *false-positive*, meaning they will detect something that is not your music. For example, they once detected a cue using the same drum loop I had used in a track. This is a perfect example of why you should always strive to make samples (and loops) your own by doing something to them so they don't sound like everyone else who is using them "straight out of the box".

As you will see from an example of their live reporting feature (figure 19-7), they list the date and time of the detection, the channel, show and episode it was played on, the duration, the number of times their service has detected this performance, the audio file which you uploaded and fingerprinted, and the ability to play the audio snippet from the show so you can hear how your music was used!

Astonishing. I once discovered that one of my cues was used on *Duck Dynasty*, but the cue never showed up on any cue sheets filed with my PRO. I determined that the cue had been attributed to another composer (it happens). Armed with this information I contacted the publisher (music library) and explained the situation and provided proof. Based on that information I got the cue sheet corrected and collected royalties from this placement. I even collected back-royalties from airings that were overlooked.

		Duration	Date/Time ▼	Channel	Show	Episode	Usage ▽expanded edit		File Path
🔅	⏱	0:24	11/02/16 01:35:25 PM	Fox Network	The Dr. Oz Show	Dr. Oz Food Investigation: The Truth About Frozen Pizza and Frozen Chicken Nuggets	⋯: No description		STO257_01_AllAmericanDoctor.wav
🔅	⏱	0:24	10/31/16 01:44:06 AM	The Hub	Leah Remini: It's All Relative	That's Life	⋯: No description	↻ 2	Pleasant_Suburbia_NO_MELODY.aif
🔅	⏱	0:15	10/31/16 01:10:05 AM	The Hub	Leah Remini: It's All Relative	That's Life	⋯: No description	↻ 2	Pleasant_Suburbia_NO_MELODY.aif
🔅	⏱	0:12	10/27/16 05:24:11 PM	E!	Keeping Up With the Kardashians	Greece Him Up	⋯: No description	↻ 6	Challenge_Accepted_FULL.aif
🔅	⏱	0:32	10/27/16 12:02:19 AM	Animal Planet	Treehouse Masters		⋯: No description	↻ 43	Desperate_Elves_FULL.aif
🔅	⏱	0:24	10/25/16 12:43:17 AM	The Hub	Leah Remini: It's All Relative	That's Life	⋯: No description	↻ 2	Pleasant_Suburbia_NO_MELODY.aif

Figure 19-7

Watermarking and Fingerprinting

There are two technologies that have been trying to become industry standard to help composers be compensated for their work. Both *watermarking* and *fingerprinting* are digital technologies to aid in identifying when music is being broadcast on TV, radio, video streaming, YouTube, etc. Both technologies have pros and cons and neither has become accepted as the best way to do this. Even within the concept, the technical approaches are handled differently between vendors.

Watermarking

A watermark is a digital signature that is embedded within the audio file. If you're familiar with photography, the name "watermark" derives from the technique of adding a symbol of some sort over a photograph so that no one else could use the image without knowing where the photograph originated from. It was a way for photographers to protect their work, often used when sharing "proofs" with customers.

In the audio world, a watermark is an audio signal that cannot be heard. This is achieved by using frequencies above the frequency range of normal human hearing. Since digital audio can go up to frequencies of 20,000 hertz and most humans cannot hear anything above 18khz (only dogs!), it's likely that those upper frequencies are used for placing watermarks.

Watermarks must be embedded into the audio file *before* it is submitted to a client in order for it to be detected.

Fingerprinting

An audio fingerprint is the mapping of digital audio that will be represented by a few numbers that makes it unique (like a social security number). This sequence of numbers - the "fingerprint" - identifies a piece of music based on the computer algorithms. With Tunesat, they can listen to just a few seconds of audio and calculate a unique identifier that can be matched with your music (because it was previously calculated and cataloged).

The benefit of this technology is that *any* music can be analyzed and calculated. Even music that was created years before this technology was invented.

Making a Living

By looking at the royalty statements above you may ask yourself, "how in the world can I expect to make a living writing music?". That's a fair question. If you only had a single piece of music placed in a show on a cable network, and it only played for 12 seconds, you won't make very much money from it. You will need to have lots and lots of music out there working for you. It is a numbers game. I've seen music I wrote 5-10 years ago *still* getting placements and still earning money. If your music is timeless you will find it being used for years to come.

Always consider the "shelf life" of music cues. Contemporary sounding cues will be great for the short term, but may not last long. Consider this when building your catalog.

The 80/20 Rule

The 80/20 rule is a principle used in general business and applies to the business of production music for TV. In essence it means, *"80% of your income will derive from 20% of your work"*. This is pretty accurate in my experience. You will create music cues that will get used over and over and over again. And it may not be your best work! Go figure. We can try to analyze why this happens, but sometimes it's just the luck of the draw.

Retirement Plan

How long should it take before you can say you're making a living from music? It will depend on how much quality music you can write and how many of those cues get placements. It's not a one-for-one formula. You could write 1,000 cues but only find placements for 50 of them. It takes time to understand how to write music that the industry wants. You'll figure it out as you go. Some people can transition in 3-5 years. Others may take up to 10 years to get to that point. If you're serious about doing this, you will make it happen.

I consider writing production music for television a great retirement plan. Not only will you receive royalties for many years to come, but those royalties can live beyond your lifetime and can benefit your descendants.

Unlike being a pop star, you don't have to be young and beautiful to be successful! This is also a job you can continue to do until the day you die. How many pop stars can say that?!

Work at a pace you feel comfortable at. There will always be a need for music.

Chapter 20 _____

PERFORMANCE RIGHTS ORGANIZATIONS (PRO)

"There is always space for improvement, no matter how long you've been in the business."
- **Oscar De La Hoya**

What is a PRO?

Performance Rights Organizations, also knowns as PROs, are the entities responsible for paying you performance royalties. Whenever your music is played in a public performance such as television, you are entitled to remuneration, i.e. a royalty, for your hard work.

If you want to get paid royalties for your work (you want to get paid, right?) you *must* join a PRO. Anyone can join ASCAP or BMI, but you must be invited to be a member of SESAC. You will want to join as both a writer and a publisher. You may not be a publisher at the moment, but it is in your best interest to become one down the line. More on this later.

In the United States, PROs include ASCAP (American Society of Composers, Authors, and Publishers), BMI (Broadcast Music, Inc.), and SESAC (Society of European Stage Authors & Composers). Outside of the U.S. you will find PRS (UK), SACEM (France), SABAM (Belgium), GEMA (Germany) and JASRAC (Japan).

*"Choosing between PROs is a matter of personal preference. ASCAP and BMI both provide the same services. One can also ask other composers for their experiences dealing with the organization, such as the registration process or member services." - **Erin M. Jacobson, music attorney***

PROs collect money from broadcasters as license fees. This gives the broadcasters the legal right to use music for their shows. The license fees will be in the form of *blanket* licenses. It would be impossible for a broadcaster to know in advance what music from which composer they plan on using during the year. The PROs filter a percentage of the collected license fees (after

covering the cost of their administrative resources) back to the composers and songwriters as royalties. The amount of money the PROs charge the broadcasters has been predetermined by a *consent decree* defined by the courts. It is intended to be fair to both parties (broadcasters and PROs).

When Does Your Music Make Money?

Anytime your music is publicly broadcast, *theoretically* you will be paid for every performance. I say "theoretically" because in practice this is impossible for the PROs to know of every instance of use of your music.

Production companies that place your music in a show - music that was supplied by yourself or a music library - are responsible for filing *cue sheets* with the PROs. A cue sheet identifies music usage on a television show. It specifies the composer's name, their PRO affiliation, the length of time the music was used, and the type of usage (theme, underscore, feature performance, etc.). Each cue sheet will contain the list of every cue used in that episode, so with reality TV it will include multiple composers, each of them belonging to different PROs (ASCAP, BMI, SESAC, etc). The cue sheets will be registered with each applicable PRO.

*"I fill out the cue sheets. I submit them to the network and the network takes care of submitting them to the PROs." - **Jen Malone, music supervisor***

Let's look at an example of a cue sheet registered with a PRO. Figures 20-2 and 20-3 below show an example of a cue sheet as filed with ASCAP:

Series Title	ASCAP Series Code	Episode Title	ASCAP Program Code
LITTLE COUPLE	54316	A MOTHERS DAY SURPRISE	2646089

∧ **Details**

Episode Number	Music Duration	Expected Air Date	Director
1	00:20:43	2013-09-03	--
Production Year	**Producer**	**Total Duration**	**Number of Episodes**
2013	--	00:30:00	1

Figure 20-2

This episode shows that the duration of the episode is 30 minutes long but the total duration of all music used is 20:43. In other words, 2/3 of the show contains music. For reality TV this number is low.

Next, let's look at a couple of the cues that were used:

Cue Sequence #: 12	Cue Title: KKF4 WORKER ANTS A	ASCAP Work ID: 883627274	Usage: B
Perf Type: BG	# of Uses: 1	Duration: 00:00:26	

BARDEN, STEVEN E
Composer Writer   ASCAP

SUM OF MUSIC
Original Publisher   ASCAP

Cue Sequence #: 13	Cue Title: KKF3 TWITCH AVENUE A	ASCAP Work ID: 883628682	Usage: B
Perf Type: BG	# of Uses: 1	Duration: 00:00:12	

BARDEN, STEVEN E
Composer Writer   ASCAP

SCORE KEEPERS MUSIC
Original Publisher

SUM OF MUSIC
Original Publisher   ASCAP

Figure 20-3

It is then the PRO's job to tally the cues and pay each composer for each performance. A cue sheet specifies the *Series and Episode* that your music played on, but not every instance when the show airs. It most likely will indicate the show's initial airing, but subsequent airings are unknown. Local TV affiliates may have syndication rights to broadcast a show any time of day on any day of the week. This is why PROs may not accurately track music performances.

With ASCAP, their "solution" is to *sample* broadcasts. They will randomly watch/listen to shows across the nation on random channels to hear what is being broadcast. Not exactly scientific. So, if you read about *watermarking* and *fingerprinting* in *Chapter 19 - How Much Money Can You Make,* you may ask, "Why can't PRO's just track every channel the way *Tunesat* does and listen for watermarks or analyze fingerprints?". Why, indeed. This would make their job easier and leave little room for error. The problem as stated in Chapter 19 is that there is not an industry standard for tracking performances. At least for now.

How each PRO handles this calculation is different, but in short: ASCAP uses the random survey and consensus method to detect performance royalties; BMI uses a scientific sampling method of tracking performances; and SESAC relies on cue sheets for TV royalties.

How Its Value Is Calculated

Each PRO has different rules for how they calculate how much money you deserve to be paid for a performance. As with ASCAP, part of their calculation depends on the time of day it is broadcast. I will reiterate again from *Chapter 19 - How Much Money Can You Make:*

- Morning (7:00am – 12:59pm) 50%
- Afternoon (1:00pm – 6:59pm) 75%
- Primetime (7:00pm – 12:59am) 100%
- Night (1:00am – 6:59am) 25%

Your royalty total is based on the number of credits you have earned for a particular placement. Credits is a designation that ASCAP uses to determine the value of the placement. The formula for calculating the credit is rather complicated, but if you're interested this is how they do it:

Use Weight x Licensee Weight x "Follow the Dollar" Factor x Time of Day Weight + Premium Credits = Total Credits

For a detailed explanation of this formula, visit the ASCAP website: *https://www.ascap.com/help/royalties-and-payment/payment/royalties*

When You'll Get Paid

ASCAP pays out royalties each month alternating the type of royalty:

- January, April, July, October: Domestic Writers
- February, May, August, November: International (Writers *and* Publishers)
- March, June, September, December: Domestic Publishers

BMI combines everything all together (Writers, Publishers, International) and pays out royalties quarterly:

- January, March, June and September

You are typically paid 9 months after the cue sheet is filed, *not* 9 months after the show airs. Sometimes cue sheets are not filed in a timely manner (it happens). I've seen royalties paid after a few years because someone dropped the ball and didn't file the cue sheets when they were supposed to.

To sum up for ASCAP and BMI, if the shows airs in the first quarter (January to March), don't expect to see a royalty payment until the fourth quarter (October, or whenever the payment period is for that type of royalty).

SESAC pays a bit quicker. Performances occurring between:

- January 1 - March 31 are distributed around (Qtr 1) June 30
- April 1 - June 30 / (Qtr 2) September 30
- July 1 - September 30 / (Qtr 3) December 31
- October 1 - December 31 / (Qtr 4) March 31 (next year)

However, for foreign royalties, money received from foreign societies between:

- January 1 - March 31 are distributed on or around September 30
- April 1 - June 30 / December 31
- July 1 - September 30 / March 31 (next year)
- October 1 - December 31 /October 1 - December 31

Writers and Publishers

Performance royalties are split evenly between the Writer (you) and the Publisher (the copyright owner). If you happen to also be the publisher then you will earn twice as much than you would if you aren't. This is why it's desirable to get your music to the client directly and avoid the middleman (the music library).

"If a composer has assigned the rights to a production company or studio, then that entity will be registering the work for copyright. If a composer retains ownership or has composed original material that (s)he then licenses, then the composer should register with the Copyright Office. Federal copyright registration comes with certain benefits – like suing for copyright infringement in federal court – which are only available to those who have a federal copyright registration."
- Erin M. Jacobson, music attorney

The music library is a broker. They work on your behalf to get your music into the hands of buyers. You may not have the resources to do this yourself. This is what their job is. By having these connections and doing the work they earn the right to collect the publisher's share. If you can do this yourself you will be that much better off.

ASCAP and BMI represent these shares differently, but it means the same thing. Don't be confused by the nomenclature. ASCAP treats royalties as a single pie with each party (writer and publisher) splitting it 50/50. BMI treats it as *two* pies (one for the writer and one for the publisher) with each pie owning 100%:

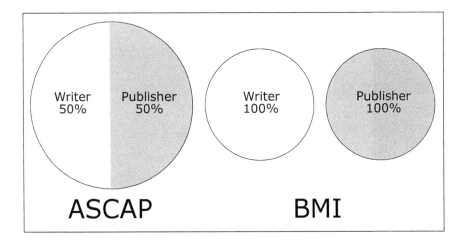

Chapter 21 _____

CONTRACTS AND OTHER LEGAL STUFF

"The entrepreneur always searches for change, responds to it, and exploits it as an opportunity." - **Peter Drucker**

Boring Stuff: Contracts

Oh, hello. I didn't expect to find you here. You probably think that a chapter on contracts will be the most boring chapter in the entire book. You're right. Contracts are boring...and confusing...and boring. Did I say boring? Nevertheless, they are extremely necessary so we need to discuss them.

Contracts are complicated and use words you wouldn't use in day-to-day conversation. I think lawyers do this on purpose to make us feel dumb. If this is how you feel about contracts, don't feel bad. You're not alone.

When you read through a contract, you'll see terms such as arbitration, hold harmless, right of first refusal, work for hire, obligations herein, full and complete consideration, blah, blah, blah.

Ugh.

Lawyers spend an enormous amount of time crafting these judicial masterpieces. Every word in a contract is important. It is complete and without ambiguity. If you end up in court there should be no question about the meaning of what you signed. It is binding and you are responsible for adhering to its content.

Why do we need contracts? To protect ourselves, our investments, and our livelihood. While a handshake or a verbal agreement may be legally binding, it is also very difficult to prove in the court of law. That's why written contracts are the only true protection you may have.

> *"What are the red flags composers should watch out for in contracts? Making sure you are not giving away rights unnecessarily and simultaneously ensuring you are getting paid fairly for the rights you are granting."* - **Erin M. Jacobson, music attorney**

CHAPTER 21 ——————————————————————————

TYPES OF CONTRACTS

For a musician, a songwriter, or a composer, the contracts you will most likely come across include:

Collaboration agreements

Songwriters working together need to decide what percentage each member will be credited with. Collaboration agreements should also designate who the point person is - i.e., the person who can make legal decisions on behalf of the team. *Appendix D* provides an example of a "Collaborators' Agreement" for a single musical work. An agreement such as this can be changed to represent a collection of songs being written for a specific project.

Work-For-Hire agreements

Also known as a *musician release,* a work-for-hire contract will be used whenever you hire a musician to perform on a recording of your composition. The purpose of the work-for-hire agreement is to show that the performer has no vested interest in the musical work. The musician is providing a service for a fee and will receive no additional payments of any kind.

If your music track or song becomes successful you do not want the hired musician(s) to claim any form of royalties due to them. Even if the musician is a close friend or family member (*especially* if a family member!) you are advised to have them sign a work-for-hire agreement.

Recording agreements

This is the agreement used by record labels. Recording agreements can be just one page but they are often complex legal documents running to many pages. These agreements apply to the recording of music only - not touring or other promotion. Typical terms include the length of the contract (in years), how much money the record company will front for recording, how many records, CDs, or downloads need to be sold before you receive any profits, etc.

This agreement falls out of the scope of writing production music for television, but occasionally an artist will become well known and transition from score/cue composer to recording artist.

Publishing agreements

There are two sides to publishing agreements: The Publisher and the *Publishee* (I made this name up!). We will leave the discussion of Publishee to the section on Music Library agreements. When you are the *Publisher*, you own the copyright to the music and will receive money - either as royalties and/or license fees - for the use of your music.

When you are in the position of placing your music directly in the hands of music buyers (music supervisors) and you haven't given up the copyright, then you are the publisher and are entitled to publisher royalties. It is important for you to register yourself (or company) as a Publishing entity with a performance rights organization (PRO) such as ASCAP, BMI, or SESAC.

Management agreements

When you get to a stage in your career when you need someone to manage your business you will sign a management agreement. Once you become too busy to handle the day-to-day business activities and just need to focus on being creative, you may decide it's time for a business manager. The specifics of what the manager will do for you is between you and the manager, but it will need to be stated in the agreement.

Band agreements

Band agreements are tricky and can vary widely. Since band members often start out as friends - not just business associates - it's important to define what each person's role is and how each member earns money. If only one or two members write all the songs, how do the remaining members make money from that? When bands become successful, that's when you find out if your agreement is fair to each party.

Music Library agreements

When you submit and place songs with a music library you will either sign an *exclusive* or *nonexclusive* agreement. If you remember from *Chapter 3 - Music Libraries,* there are pros and cons to both exclusive and nonexclusive arrangements. However, if you sign with a particular music library you may not be given a choice whether their agreements are one or the other.

By assigning your music to a music library you entrust them with the job of finding placements for your music in film and TV. In return for this the music libraries usually insist on taking 100% of the Publishing and will now own the copyright. Since they are now the *publisher*, they are entitled to the Publisher's royalties. This makes you the *Publishee.*

In recent years, many television production companies have insisted on being the publisher of your music. This has left the music libraries no other choice than to require that you, the composer, allocate a percentage (up to 25%) of the Writer's share to them. This is the only way the music library can make any money in that circumstance since they are no longer the publisher. Whether this is right or wrong for TV production companies to make this demand, this has been happening. TV productions companies have found a way to make extra money. As a composer, you have a choice to deny the music library's request and take your business elsewhere or give up a portion of your Writer's share.

> *"Sync fees can be highly negotiable, but it's unethical, and in some cases illegal, for production companies to demand what is in essence a kickback."*
> *- Jeff Rona, Liquid Cinema*

"We discourage that. I think it's unethical. Composers are entitled to what composers are entitled to. If a production company wants to have a share of that writer's work then they need to set up their own publishing company and sign that composer on as a composer to that publishing company. This is the legitimate way to do this. 'Pay-to-play' is wrong."
- Edwina Travis-Chin, APM Music

Here is an example of a real contract where the library owner insists on taking 50% of the writer's share. This is not because a TV production company has demanded the publishing. It is also vague regarding when this will occur.

"As [name withheld] (as an individual) is music director for COMPANY and participates in changing and/or re-writing any Master or Material, COMPANY will accord 50% of the writer's share of public performance royalties to Copyright Owner and [name withheld] will be accorded the remaining 50% of writer's share of The Works. "

This is vague because it states "and participates", not "if participates". When encountering contracts such as this, please know of the potential pitfalls. Remember to consult an attorney when unsure.

Besides the royalties you will earn on the back end, you may also be entitled to a share of the license (or *sync*) fees. Most libraries will split the license fee 50/50 with you. But with blanket license fees, expect no money. This is because of the ridiculous amount of bookkeeping involved to figure out how to split the fees with all of the composers involved. If you were licensing a single track for a specific placement, you would split the license fee with the library for that one license. Blanket licenses are different. A music library is delivering hundreds or thousands of tracks for a blanket fee. This blanket fee covers the use of all of the music tracks. But there is no guarantee that all of the tracks will ever get used. It becomes impossible to figure out how to fairly distribute the blanket license fee amongst all of the composers.

Refer to *Appendix E, F, and G* for examples of exclusive and nonexclusive music library agreements. You will notice how different each one is. Every music library has their contract crafted for their specific needs.

Common Contract Elements

You probably noticed how different the content of each of the contract examples were from *Appendix E, F, and G*. Although they varied in length and substance, there are many common elements between all of them. When perusing a contract for details, you will become familiar with the many *boilerplate* areas and the more specific sections related to the contract in question.

> *"If you do get asked to write for, or place existing music with a library, read the contract. Not all deals are the same, and some libraries are far better than others in terms of business." - **Jeff Rona, Liquid Cinema***

Specifics

These are the most common items you will find in the contracts that musicians, songwriters, and composers will be involved with.

- **Rights**

  The rights you grant the company defines what they are getting from you and vice-versa. It will define the percentage of ownership or royalty or license splits between each party, and stating how they may change or alter your music to fit their needs. It may also state whether the contract is an exclusive or nonexclusive agreement.

  This clause is very important to understand because it becomes the basis of what the company will do for you and what you will get out of it.

- **Term**

This defines how long the contract is good for. It is stated in years. For music library contracts a term of 2 - 5 years is common. Know that contracts often state that the term will automatically renew for another year at a time unless they hear from you - in writing - prior to the deadline.

- **Territory**

Where the contract is applicable. To be on the safe side this usually covers *worldwide*, but if that's not big enough they also specify the *universe*.

- **Compensation**

How much money you will earn from the company is very important. This section will define how license fees will be split (if at all) and what percentage of both the writer's and publisher's share of royalties you are entitled to.

- **Warranties and Representation**

This section confirms that you are free and clear to sign the agreement and promise that all of the music you create is original and no one else is making any claims against you and your music.

Boilerplate

These are items found in most contracts. They are not specific to the agreement but outline common legal clauses.

- **Accounting and Audit Rights**

Understanding how a company handles money - particularly when it's yours - is important to know. Most contracts specify when and how you can audit their books to make sure you're being paid what you're owed.

- **Indemnification**

Companies want to ensure that you will not sue them if something goes wrong, or if a third party sues you, you can't turn around and sue the company.

- **Notices**

Any time the company needs to send you any notices of any kind - payments, contracts, Christmas cards - will go to the address given in the information section. You are responsible for keeping the company up to date with any address changes. Make sure they can find you to send you money.

- **Modification**

You are not allowed the change the content of the agreement without first writing a letter to the company requesting the change which both parties must agree to. So, for example, if the term of the contract is for five years, you can't decide on your own that you want it to be three years.

- **Assignment**

If the company sells their business they may assign over any of the business holdings - including you! - to the next assignee.

- **Arbitration**

Nobody wants to go to court and pay expensive lawyers. Arbitration is less painful way to resolve legal problems and most companies insist on this method. Arbitration rulings are as binding as any court ruling.

When to Contact an Attorney

Contracts can be very confusing. This information has given you an overview of what type of information is contained within most contracts. Although the wording may vary, the ideas are consistent.

When looking at a contract and you don't understand *exactly* what is being stated, seek advice from an attorney. I know attorneys can be expensive, so you may ask yourself, *"is it worth it?"*. Initially this expense may not seem to makes sense. But over the lifetime of your music it will. If you make a poor decision and sign a contract that takes advantage of you, you will have wasted even more money in the long run than those original attorney fees.

Also, check out various legal web sites such as RocketLawyer.com, LegalZoom.com, and many others. Just remember, legal advice - as with many other things in life - you get what you pay for.

> *"To find an attorney, one can ask for referrals from composer friends, composer or songwriter organizations, or even Google. Be sure to interview the attorney first to make sure the relationship seems like the right fit."*
> **- Erin M. Jacobson, music attorney**

Chapter 22 _____

YOUR MUSIC AS A BUSINESS

"There are no secrets to success. It is the result of preparation, hard work, and learning from failure." - **Colin Powell**

This is a Business!

Once you earn money from writing music you have a business. That means you are responsible for paying taxes on any money you earn. For many people being a business owner is a scary proposition. Even if you are the only employee you must adhere to the business laws of your city, county, state, and Federal government.

This also means you need to become (or stay) organized. Refer to *Chapter 18 - Organizing Your Life* if you need a refresher. Recordkeeping is a must - not only for declaring deductions but in the case of a tax audit.

If you have employees (a good problem to have) you will be responsible for payroll taxes, business insurance, health insurance, etc. At this stage, you will want to employ an office manager and/or accountant to handle all of these mundane but necessary tasks.

Recordkeeping

Whether you throw everything in a shoe box or use modern bookkeeping software to track your purchases and activities, you must save everything related to your business. Buy a sample library? Save the receipt. Buy a new computer? Save the receipt. Take a client out for a business lunch? Save the receipt. How many miles did your drive for that business lunch? Write that number down.

Saving receipts is one of many routines you need to follow regularly. Anything that might be construed as business-related is a candidate for including in your shoe box. We will discuss the things you can use for deductions shortly.

Business Licenses

Do you need a business license to run your business? That depends on local ordinances. If your city or county or even your state requires you to have a business license then it's in your best interest to comply. Penalties for ignoring this requirement can be substantial whereas the cost of the business license may be minimal. If you earn money from providing a service then you are considered a business and must comply with these rules - even if you run your business out of your garage.

What are the costs of a business license? As an example, if you are a "creative artist" in Los Angeles County the annual cost of the license is based on a percentage of your income unless it's under $300,000 which in that case there is no tax to be paid. But if you fail to acquire the license then you will be penalized substantially! It's not worth taking a chance. Besides, the cost of this business license will be a deduction on your tax return.

The initial cost of the license will also vary from state to state. For example, Alaska will charge about $50 whereas Nevada charges $200.

Tax Returns

When you earn money, the Federal government will want their fair share of your earnings. Failure to declare any income and file taxes for it could earn you substantial penalties (not to mention landing you in prison!). It's not worth the risk. As long as your record keeping is accurate then you may claim many deductions against this income.

The next question you may ask is whether to file taxes for your business as a sole proprietor, a partnership, a corporation (subchapter S or C), or an LLC (limited liability company). There are pros and cons for deciding how to treat your business from a legal standpoint. A company will be an S-Corp or LLC to protect their personal assets in the case of lawsuits. This discussion is beyond the scope of this book. Please contact an attorney before deciding which way to file.

*"When a composer should incorporate depends on a variety of factors, mostly regarding liability and tax. Each composer's situation is different, so a composer should speak with his or her lawyer and CPA to determine whether the liability protection is needed and whether the tax implications are helpful or hindering." - **Erin M. Jacobson, music attorney***

Types of Deductions

There are many types of deductions you can legitimately claim and you should take every possible advantage of them. Remember to keep copies of all receipts when you purchase something. We all buy stuff online these days so save the emails containing those receipts.

Here are some of the categories of items that can and should be taken as deductions:

- **Musical instruments and accessories**
Guitars, strings, wood polish, wah-wah pedal, MIDI devices, etc.

- **Music software**
Your DAW software, notation software (Finale and Sibelius), and any other music-related software

- **Sample libraries**

- **Bookkeeping software**
Any financial software such as Quicken, recordkeeping tools such as Excel

- **Computer hardware**
Includes desktop and laptop computers, disk drives (hard drives and SSD), printers, ink, paper, monitors, MIDI interfaces

- **Research materials**

This is a broad category. Anything you use to help you stay informed about the music business, musical trends, etc.:
- o CDs
- o Music streaming services
- o DVDs, Blu-rays, movies rentals, theater tickets
- o Cable TV subscription
- o Netflix, HULU, HBO, Amazon Prime, etc.
- o Sheet music
- o Music books of any nature

- **Education**

Any continuing education (field related), online courses, seminars

- **Industry events**

Conferences, film screenings

- **Industry memberships**

This can include membership into any organization that promotes your business or provides a service to further your career

- **Travel expenses**

Gas, mileage, vehicle service, DMV fees, hotel, meals, airfare, taxi, train, hot air balloon, etc.

- **Home-In-Office**

This is a great deduction but this only works if your studio/office space is used 100% for your business. With this you figure out the percentage of your home that your business space takes up and apply this same percentage on your mortgage/rent, utilities, insurance, etc.

If you're not sure about whether something is a deduction or not, save the receipt! Ask your accountant or tax preparer if you're unclear. If you're preparing and filing your own taxes you may have missed out on some deductions. An experienced tax person will know the right questions to ask you. In my experience, it's worth the cost of hiring a professional to handle this complicated task. Besides, the cost of hiring this professional is a tax deduction on its own.

Part 5

Networking and Social Media

Chapter 23 _____

PROMOTING YOUR MUSIC THROUGH SOCIAL MEDIA

"If people like you, they'll listen to you, but if they trust you, they'll do business with you."
- **Zig Ziglar**

Using Social Media

Social media is often thought of as a tool for artists: musicians, songwriters, performers, and the like to promote their music and become well known. But what about for music production composers? Is there any point in trying to promote your music the same way? Of course there is.

The reason for promoting your music may not the same as for artists. In most cases, you are not promoting your latest CD (album, song, etc.) hoping to rack up sales numbers. With production music composers, your goal is to get your music known to those who can get your music placed in television, film, and commercials.

Your target: Music supervisors, music libraries, filmmakers, and ad agencies. All of these companies (and individuals) will have a Facebook page. They may also indulge in Twitter, LinkedIn, Snapchat, Instagram, and any other social media platform that is popular today.

Follow or "friend" them on those platforms. With Facebook and Twitter, you can promote your music by posting audio links (SoundCloud, BandCamp, SoundClick, etc.) or video links (YouTube).

> *"Every so often I come across a composer online whose work impresses me enough to reach out."* - **Jeff Rona, Liquid Cinema**

Both Facebook and LinkedIn feature "groups" that target various communities such as music composers for media. Almost any group can be located. This give you a good way to interact with like-minded individuals. Try to find groups that contain filmmakers, music supervisors, video game developers, and others that would have a use for your music.

Remember that social networking on the Internet is not much different than interacting in person. Get to know people before bombarding them with your music. Give them a reason to ask you for examples of your music. Nobody likes to have your business shoved in theirs. Be considerate. Instead, take the opportunity to cultivate friendships.

On your own Facebook and Twitter page you can promote your music tracks and brag about your latest accomplishments. As you gain followers you will have a built-in audience. Your goal by following (or friending) those targeted companies and individuals is for them to reciprocate and follow you back. When this happens, you will have a better chance of them getting to know what you do.

Tools of the Trade

Understanding social media and how to promote your music is key. Posting willy-nilly will not target followers efficiently. There are scientific studies (analytics) that have defined how to best promote your business:

- **Facebook**
  Best days to post: Thursday and Friday
  Most shares: 1 pm
  Most likes: 3 pm

- **Twitter**
  Best days to post: Wednesday, Saturday, and Sunday
  Most retweets: 1 pm
  Best CTR (click-thru rate): 12 pm and 6 pm

- **YouTube**

Best days to post: Thursday thru Sunday
Best time to post: 12 pm to 3 pm
Worst time to post: 5 pm to 6 pm

- **Instagram**

Best days to post: Monday
Best time to post: 3 pm to 4 pm
Consistent engagement 7 days a week

Twitter has introduced *Periscope* for live broadcasting and Facebook followed suit by introducing *Facebook Live*. Expect more of this social interaction in the future.

Consider using tools such as Crowdfire and Hootsuite. They allow you to connect all (or most) of your social accounts and post in-advance so you don't have to monitor when to post something. They also offer analytics to help you evaluate how many eyeballs you're getting on each post and how followers are interacting with you (retweets, shares, likes, etc.).

Don't forget to use hashtags (#) with keywords that help drive people to your page. As with metadata when submitting to music libraries, don't over-tag or spam tags that are not applicable to your business. Using a hashtag like *#FreeMoney* will do you no good unless you are offering free money to people. If that's the case, let me know!

Building Your Credibility

By having an Internet presence on social media, you will build up not only a following but credibility. As word of mouth spreads, you will gain more and more followers who will be eager to hear your latest music tracks.

You never know where your next placement will come from. For example, you might have a SoundCloud follower who is a huge fan of your music. This follower may know someone who needs music for a film project or an ad campaign. Since this follower knows your music they may recommend you to that person. Word of mouth is a powerful networking tool.

Chapter 24 _____

NETWORKING

"At the end of the day it's all based on relationships." - **Jen Malone**

Why Network?

This is a people business. Personal relationships are the key to getting anywhere. This is not unique to our industry. This is true no matter what business you are in. The more people in the business you know the better your chances of succeeding.

We have become an online world. There is more interaction with people over the Internet than there is in person. This is a problem. Your perception of someone is different when you only know them "online" versus in person. If you've "known" someone online for a while and then meet them in person, you end up having a different opinion of them later on because you've made a personal connection with them.

This distinction is important and makes a difference how you conduct business with people. We've discussed how it is possible to live anywhere in the world and still succeed in this business. But if you network with people in person, your success rate will increase.

So now the question is, who are these people and where do you go to meet them?

> *"The important thing to understand about networking is that it is not to simply add names and numbers to your rolodex. Networking is to learn to know people and build relationships. Usually that is where my new opportunities come from – from friendships."* - **Lydia Ashton, composer**

Who to Network With

In *Chapter 23 - Promoting Your Music Through Social Media*, we discussed the importance of connecting with people through social media:

Facebook, Twitter, LinkedIn, etc. These social network sites are important for making connections with these people, but how do you know who these people are to begin with?

Let's start with music supervisors. We already know building a relationship with a music supervisor is the best way to get your music into TV and film. Without a direct relationship with a music supervisor you must depend on music libraries to act as a broker and work on your behalf to get your music to them.

But who are they? At the end of every film and TV show the credits will list the names of everyone involved in the show or film. If watching TV, you can pause the show on your DVR (if you don't have a DVR, get one!). But if you're watching a film in a theater and can't pause it then you can try IMDB. The Internet Movie DataBase is a crowd-sourced repository so the information is not always 100% accurate.

Armed with this information you can then search for these individuals on Facebook, Twitter, LinkedIn, etc. Then follow the steps as outlined in Chapter 23 to interact with them.

Next is music libraries. Start with Googling "music libraries" or refer to other resources like the web site *Music Library Report*. Once you find a music library then you can just go to their own web site. The music library may also have Facebook and Twitter accounts, but at this point you're only dealing with the library in general, not a specific person.

If the music library's web site does not contain an "About Us" page then you may not know who the actual people are who run the company. I have found that searching LinkedIn is a good resource for tracking down individuals who work for the company. Just search for the company and it will reveal a list of employees working there.

Where to Go

To meet these people in person you will probably need to be in areas like Los Angeles, New York, and even Nashville. Los Angeles is the mecca for the film and TV industry. These cities are where most of the industry events take place. If you want to meet these people in person you must be physically there.

> *"I've also met several excellent composers at panels and workshops, as well as simply getting emails from them." - **Jeff Rona, Liquid Cinema***

These are many of the industry events and conferences that occur in these major cities:

- **ASCAP**
ASCAP Expo

- **PMA (Production Music Association)**
Production Music Conference (PMC)

- **CCC (California Copyright Conference)**
Various conferences throughout the year

- **Vegas Music Summit**
Held in Las Vegas

- **Taxi A&R**
Taxi Road Rally

- **AIMP (Association of Independent Publishers)**
Various conferences throughout the year

- **SXSW**

Held in Austin, TX

- **Game Developers Conference**

For video game developers, but useful for composers

- **MUSEXPO**

Covers panels for artists and media composers

- **NAB (National Association of Broadcasters)**

Shows in Las Vegas and New York

- **SCL (Society of Composers & Lyricists)**

Conferences and panels throughout the year

There are many other organizations holding smaller conferences throughout the year all across the United States, Canada, and Europe. Besides these various conferences, look up "meetup" groups in your area. These are not groups for *hot singles.* These are groups for industry professionals to meet and network with.

When you attend an industry event your goal is to meet and have a conversation with someone in the industry that can help you move your career to the next level. How will you do this? Do you have a plan? Are you comfortable walking up to a stranger and striking up a conversation without sounding aggressive or desperate? This kind of approach is akin to a "cold call" sales call. It rarely turns out well.

Let's start with who you will meet. What do you know about this person? Other than their job title and the company they work with, what do you know about them? I assume you've selected this person to talk to because you knew that this person would be there and/or on a discussion panel. If you want to make a good impression, know some significant facts about this person.

Spend time ahead of the event to do research about this person's professional background. At the least, know what shows this person has worked on. This way you can at least mention that show as a point of discussion. If you liked the show and/or what they contributed to it, let them know. If you try to bullshit them they will know it. Be sincere. Don't discuss something and pretend you know something you don't.

These industry professionals at these events are in high demand. If they've just come off of a panel you can expect 20 or 30 people to surround them and try to converse with them. If you've ever experienced this you know how annoying it is when one person monopolizes the conversation and never stops talking. Not only are other people waiting to speak with them, you don't want to overstay your welcome. That's not how to make a good impression. Be brief, succinct, and cordial. Get to your point and move on. This is where we come to the *15-second elevator pitch.*

Your 15-Second Elevator Pitch

The 15-second elevator pitch is the hypothetical scenario where you run across someone you wanted to meet while stepping onto an elevator. You don't know how far this person will travel so you need to be quick! What are you going to say in that short timespan that has meaning, is memorable, and covers everything you need to say? Think of the 15-second pitch as the equivalent of the 140-character limit of a Twitter tweet. In fact, Twitter is a good way to practice creating this short sales pitch since the average tweet takes between 10 and 15 seconds to read.

You're selling your brand - what you do as a composer - the same way you would sell a product like soap. The basic structure of the pitch is the headline followed by 3 bullet points. Short and succinct. If you have more time then you can expand on the bullet points. The key is to craft your headline to be attention grabbing.

To define your headline, ask yourself "What is the single most important thing I want my listener to know about my product/service/ brand/idea?" For example, I might say "I specialize in composing music for reality TV". It's short and succinct. Because it includes "composing music" the listener understands that I compose music. But because I emphasized "specialize" and "reality TV" the listener understands that not only do I compose music but I must be really good at reality TV music because it's my specialty. It also implies that I also compose music in other styles and for other mediums.

For my bullet points I might include "I work with clients to provide them with quirky styles they don't have access to", or "Clients love the level of realism in my orchestral sounds". You don't want to brag. You're trying to sell your services so you want to make it enticing. You're selling the sizzle - not the steak!

After you've crafted the perfect pitch, write it down and practice it. Practice it over and over until it becomes natural and doesn't sound like you've memorized a speech or sound like an infomercial. You also don't want to recite it too fast or you'll end up sounding like Ralphie from "A Christmas Story" who wanted "an Official Red Ryder Carbine-Action Two-Hundred-Shot Range Model Air Rifle with a compass in the stock!"

That's a sure-fire way to shoot your eye out.

Building Your Reputation

This is a business built around relationships. It's all about people. It's also a small community. Music supervisors and music library folks attend the same conferences as one another and they know each other. As you get to know these people it's critical that you maintain a level of professionalism throughout your business activities with them. This is your reputation.

CHAPTER 24 ——————————————————————————

*"There needs to be an element of trust. It's been a process of meeting people and forming those relationships." - **Jen Malone, music supervisor***

People talk. When these folks get together at the various conferences they like to tell each other stories about their recent experiences in the business, and this includes meeting people like you. When one of their encounters goes awry, it will be a story that will be shared amongst their peers.

It's important to maintain a level of professionalism and never be annoying. You may meet a music supervisor who might not be having a great day. It happens. When it does it's possible they may not be the most congenial person they normally are at that moment. Try to "read the room" and understand if this is one situation where you need to back off. Everybody's allowed to have a bad day.

There will always be another day to make network connections with folks. In fact, the more often you attend industry events the more times you will run into these people. Get to know them a little bit at a time. You will have more success by just getting to know them as people before you push your music on them. They know you have music to sell - that's why you're attending that event.

WRITING PRODUCTION MUSIC FOR TV

Chapter 25 _____

FINDING OTHER OUTLETS FOR YOUR MUSIC

"Music is the universal language of mankind." - **Henry Wadsworth Longfellow**

Making Money Outside of TV

Whether you have found success or not placing your music in television shows, there are still additional ways to earn money with your music tracks. While scoring a film is one way to make money writing music, this is not the same as production music cues. Custom film scores are written to fit the action on the screen *exactly*. Production music cues stand alone on their own and can be used in a variety of ways

Think of it this way: Production music is *reusable* music; Film score music is unique and specific to a film.

These are, of course, generalizations. Many cues written as part of a film score could be repurposed in a *production music* way. By the same token, many production music cues could be part of a film score.

> *"Try not to make your music generic. It has to sound authentic."*
> *- Jen Malone, music supervisor*

Let's take a look at some alternatives to the production music market. These represent many of the more accessible music markets.

- **Television Commercials**

  Having your music cue or song in a National television spot can earn you tens, if not hundreds of thousands of dollars. The larger the spot, the more difficult it will be to get your music placed in a commercial. Difficult, but not impossible. Like with everything else, if you know someone within an ad agency it will increase your chances of exposure and landing one of these lucrative placements.

There are many opportunities for placing your music in local and regional commercial spots. These smaller spots are usually handled by much smaller advertising agencies. These agencies are more accessible at this level. You may even get in touch with local mattress stores or car dealerships that advertise in your local market. Everything you can do to build your resume is valid.

● Radio Commercials

Besides TV spots, radio is still a viable medium. Radio commercials also need music. Just like television, radio advertisers create advertising and marketing campaigns using advertising agencies. The same rules apply here: Smaller ad campaigns will use smaller ad agencies

Radio stations themselves use music jingles throughout the year. They may use music tracks from music libraries (just as TV shows do), but many times they will need something custom written for a special promotion they're doing.

● Video Games

Video game composing is the new film scoring. Soundtracks for video games have gone from simple 8-bit beeps and blips to full-size orchestral scores. Many of the score for games are as good if not better than many film scores.

Writing music for video games shares a similarity to writing for music production libraries: You are still writing music that triggers an emotional response from the audience (or player). It also shares a similarity to that of film scoring: You are writing a cue that fits a general setting in the game. It could be a battle or a car chase.

What makes game composing different than either of those is the structure of the composition. Video game music loops. The player could be stuck on a level for hours at a time. It may not be as simple as writing an A-B-A form. The music must loop seamlessly. When the cue ends, it must start over with no noticeable break. This is a necessary skill for the game composer.

And just like production music, game music comprises *stems*. Variations of the music will cross-fade in and out as the player moves from one part of the scene to another. The cue may break down to just drums and percussion and later bring in brass stabs. The decision to change stems on the fly comes from the programmers designing the game. Certain actions within the game will cause musical variations to support the scene and excite the player.

Tools such as FMod, Wwise, and Unreal take the guesswork out of how to make this happen, but you need to compose music in an intelligent manner to make it succeed.

● Mobile Apps

Mobile apps for iOS and Android devices can sometimes use original music, but mostly these needs are relegated to games. There are thousands of independent game developers trying to make it big and become a runaway hit (like *Angry Birds* and *Flappy Bird*). A few become huge while the rest languish in obscurity. Regardless of their success, most of them need music.

The same concepts for composing video game music for mobile devices is the same as for the AAA games, albeit with much smaller budgets. By gaining experience in the mobile game market you can build up your resume and this experience can land you a prominent gig with a major video game maker.

● Corporate Videos

A corporate video can be anything from a training video from a company's HR department to a wedding video. Since the budgets for these types of projects are miniscule they will most often resort to using music from a royalty-free music library. But that's not always the case. They may seek something special that is not easily found in your typical music library, so this is your chance to make a new friend and become indispensable.

● **Documentaries**

Documentaries are somewhere between a corporate video and a small feature film as far as the budgets go. Documentaries can be scored by a composer the same way you would write to picture for a feature film. Depending on the subject in a documentary the music they use can range from custom score, to stock library cues, to licensed songs (famous or not). Many composers enjoy writing for documentaries because they often have a more *artistic* side to them. Studios that produce documentaries are not looking to create sales from the soundtrack album from their films. The music may often be more compelling than a commercial film project would.

● **Independent Films**

An independent film is a film that does not have the same corporate financial backing that supports major films. Not to demean feature films put out by major film studios, but independent films are often the creation of a single filmmaker with an artistic vision who finances the film through independent channels and crowd-sourced funding. The filmmaker's primary goal is not to become the biggest blockbuster of all time.

● **Student Films**

A student film is just what is sounds like. Film school students will produce at least one or two films over the course of their education. These films typically range from 8 to 30 minutes. Everyone involved is a newbie and it's a great way to learn the craft of writing music to picture. Not only that, you never know what long-term relationships you may make when working on student films. After all, no one knows who the next Steven Spielberg will be!

- **Web Sites**

    Believe or not, you can find work writing music for a web site. A site may have an intro page that needs some delightful music or may have instructional material that is set to music (think *corporate video*). Even though these opportunities are not as plentiful as some of the others I've mentioned, they exist.

- **Podcasts**

    In a much smaller scale than television and radio, podcasts are becoming more and more relevant and every one of those shows need at least a theme song. Podcasts were once the domain of unknown broadcasters, but are now becoming an outlet for major celebrities to entertain and share their message with the world.

Where to Find These Outlets

I hope you understand that there are many different outlets for your music outside of the TV and film market. You need to be creative. It was not too long ago that you could earn a little extra money writing on-hold music for company's voice mail systems. New and exciting musical opportunities are invented all the time. Community theatre might need *incidental* music that plays between scenes. Theme Parks need music for their attractions. Traveling circuses and carnivals are not as prevalent as they once were, but something new always comes along to replace them. Explore the many possibilities.

Networking will always produce better results than flipping through the phone book to find your next client. Any of the methods discussed in *Chapter 24 - Networking* are a good place to find who holds the keys to your next kingdom.

LinkedIn and Facebook groups are a good way to find people who work in advertising, video game creators, web site developers...you name it! Join in the community discussions and get to know these people. Find out who are the people you should target for making a great connection in that industry. Remember, many of the folks there are beginners and are learning about that business, so they may not be the best people to connect with - at least for the time being.

One last important option to consider: Build your own music library. This is a lot tougher than it sounds. Once you've gained enough experience working with existing music libraries you might start your own business. After you've made connections with music supervisors you can supply them with thousands of your *own* tracks (along with music from a roster of composers writing for *you*). Like any other business, make sure you understand it from all aspects before you go down this road. It's more than writing music, but the benefits can be life changing. Good luck!

Part 6

Epilogue

Chapter 26 _____

WHERE DO I GO FROM HERE?

"I live cinema and passionately love music, and my efforts in both these crafts are unfolding." - **Priyanka Chopra**

Long Term Goals

If you've ever sat in a job interview you may have faced the question, *"Where do you see yourself in 5 years?"*. This is a valid question as it gives the interviewer an idea of whether you'll continue to grow or just be complacent and stagnate. The same question applies to this business: Where do you see yourself in 5 years, 10 years, or even 25 years?

If you can't answer this question just yet, don't worry. But you need to think about it. I want you to find the road to success. As George Harrison once sang, *"If you don't know where you're going, any road will take you there"*. Do you want to grow musically and financially or will you be happy being complacent? What level of success will make you happy? Do you want to make a living doing this or are you fine with making this a part-time job? How many pieces of music do you want or expect to write per year? How much money do you want to make each year? How many music libraries do you want to be part of? How many tracks within each music library do you want to provide?

> *"When you do get your music into a library, be very patient. It can take months or even years for a track to get discovered, get used, get some fees and royalties in place, and start to see income."* - **Jeff Rona, Liquid Cinema**

Whether you keep this information in your head or create a spreadsheet you'll need metrics to gauge your progress. For example, if you've said your goal is to write 3 music cues per week and you come up short you may need to change your plan to be more realistic. You want to push yourself to reach these goals, but there's no point in stressing yourself out over it. Figure out

WRITING PRODUCTION MUSIC FOR TV

what's a comfortable goal and work within those parameters.

Assess your progress to see if you need to step up your work or change your plan. Limit this to only 3 or 4 times a year. Micro-managing yourself can have negative impact on your results. Give yourself some breathing room and step back to look at your progress. If you're good at making charts you can see your progress in a visual way. The idea is to keep you motivated to reach your goal.

Education / Keep Studying

Is it possible to know everything there is to know about the music business? Possibly, but not likely. There is always something new to learn. This makes it exciting! Things change, technology evolves, styles that are popular today become unpopular tomorrow...and then become popular again for the next generation.

> *"Be a sponge. Take any opportunity you have to learn and improve, whether it is in this area or other areas of life. Read books, watch tutorials, learn from colleagues, and learn from trial and error. You have never "arrived" – there is always more to learn." -* **Lydia Ashton, composer**

Writing music for television is a journey. It's constantly changing and so should you. You don't want to fall into that rut of producing the same music over and over again. At some point it may stop working for you. You must stay current on many fronts. Here are things to think about.

Striving to be better should always be your goal: Being a better composer; A better recording engineer; A better business person; A better human being...these are all important goals. Do these things happen over time organically or do you have to reach out to learn these things and better yourself? Many things get better just by experience, doing things over and over until you perfect them. For example, take audio engineering. You can improve your skills at doing this by trial-and-error. Learn from your mistakes. Try different ways of doing things until it's better.

Other areas may need formal training. Taking classes at your local community college, at the university, online, private lessons...any way you can gain knowledge from a professional is worth your while. Whether you need training with music theory, or business fundamentals, you can find what you're looking for.

YouTube is a vast resource for learning new things. This information may not be as organized as a formal classroom lecture, but good information is out there. Check out some online courses. Apple has created *ITunes U* through their App Store to allow you to take classes from universities such as Stanford, Harvard, Yale, Ohio State, University of Oxford, Penn State, and others.

Watch a lot of TV. Seriously. If you want to write music for TV you need to know the types of music they're using. This is part of *understanding what the industry needs.* Pay attention to how emotion is being used in the music. If you want to understand emotion, learn about acting. As a student of film scoring I was encouraged to study acting to have a better understanding of the craft and to learn how emotion is conveyed. It seems like this would have nothing to do with music, but it does. Good actors can suck you into a scene and make you believe in the character they're portraying and the emotional impact they give. The same thing happens with music. Music is just another character in the scene.

Conferences

Chapter 24 - Networking provided suggestions for various music conferences that occur throughout the year. Not only are they great opportunities for networking they are also educational. Most of the conferences feature panels discussing various aspects of the music industry such as copyright issues, royalties, music licensing, and more. Try to go to as many of these conferences as possible.

"I go to conventions from time to time. I especially like the PMC conference. It's focused on production music. The topics and the level of the panelists are much higher than you would find at a more generic music conference."
- Matt Hirt, composer

Networking is always an important goal for any of these events, but don't overlook the educational aspect. Try to learn something from every event you attend. If the panels also include *music pitches* - an opportunity to have your music listened to by the panelists (often music supervisors) - take every advantage of this. You may learn something about the effectiveness of your music track in respect to the panelists' needs. Not only from your own tracks but from every music cue pitched by an audience member. Learn why the panel loved or hated each track and how they might use it in their own job.

Following Trends

Every industry has trends: music, fashion, automobiles, you name it. Musical trends change rapidly. A huge part of the production music industry is having music available that sounds like the latest hit by whatever popular artist is topping the charts this week.

This will be ongoing over your entire career. Over my lifetime, I've lived through folk music, the British invasion, acid rock, Disco, progressive rock, punk, electronica, New Wave, saxophones are in, saxophones are out, rap, Hip Hop, etc. It never ends.

You may not be interested in learning every style that becomes popular, but at least have a familiarity with these styles so you can make intelligent decisions about whether you should invest your time in learning one style or another.

Television will always want current styles. It keeps their shows relevant. The more current styles you can produce the more your chances will increase of getting placements.

Recap

Throughout this book, I've emphasized the importance of understanding emotion. Emotion is the cornerstone of writing music for film and TV. Every note you write means something. By deciding to move a note in an upward direction instead of going downward, you can control the emotion you're trying to convey.

No matter what style of music you write, you are writing an emotion. Understanding this basic concept will help guide you as you embark on this journey. It will aid in developing a roadmap for your compositions and eliminate any conflicting message your music is trying to say.

Just as important as understanding emotion is understanding what the industry wants. Don't be the square peg that doesn't fit in the round hole. Listen to what's going on in television *today*. Tomorrow may be a different, just as yesterday was different. Stay current and stay relevant.

Keep your gear up to date if possible, but more importantly, stay current with your sample libraries. The bar is *very* high in terms of sound quality and authenticity. Don't expect that to change any time soon. If you can record your music using real instruments instead of sampled ones - do it!

You will experience many successes throughout your career and many disappointments. Take these negative experiences in stride. Never take rejection personally. Use it as a learning tool to turn that negative into a positive.

I hope the information I've presented in this book serves you well. Because of the nature of this business many of the topics described here may not be this way by the time you get there. Although this information is fundamentally sound, use your own judgement as the need arises.

Happy composing and good luck!

Glossary

Ad Agency
An advertising agency, often referred to as a creative agency, is a business dedicated to creating, planning, and handling advertising and sometimes other forms of promotion and marketing for its clients.

Algorithm
A process or set of rules to be followed in calculations or other problem-solving operations, especially by a computer.

Algorithmic Composition
Algorithmic composition is the technique of using algorithms to create music. Algorithms (or, at the very least, formal sets of rules) have been used to compose music for centuries; the procedures used to plot voice-leading in Western counterpoint, for example, can often be reduced to algorithmic determinacy.

Artificial Intelligence
The theory and development of computer systems able to perform tasks that normally require human intelligence, such as visual perception, speech recognition, decision-making, and translation between languages.

ASCAP
The American Society of Composers, Authors and Publishers is an American not-for-profit performance-rights organization (PRO) that protects its members› musical copyrights by monitoring public performances of their music, whether via a broadcast or live performance, and compensating them accordingly. See also *PRO*.

GLOSSARY

Audio Bus

A mixing path allowing audio signals to be combined into a single sound source to create 'sub mixes'.

Backend

Performance royalties are paid several months after the music has been placed and performed in a public performance. The opposite being payments being paid 'up front', usually in the form of a license fee.

Bass Trap

Bass traps are acoustic energy absorbers which are designed to damp low frequency sound energy with the goal of attaining a flatter low frequency (LF) room response by reducing LF resonances in rooms.

Blanket License

A type of license allowing a music user, typically a TV network, or radio station, to play or perform all compositions covered under the license without a limit on use for one (usually annual) payment. PROs and Production Libraries often use blanket licenses with television, Film, and radio stations.

BMI

Broadcast Music, Inc. is an American not-for-profit performance-rights organization (PRO) that protects its members› musical copyrights by monitoring public performances of their music, whether via a broadcast or live performance, and compensating them accordingly. See also *PRO*.

BPM

Beats per minute (bpm) is a unit typically used as a measure of tempo in music and heart rate. The bpm tempo of a piece of music is conventionally shown in its score as a metronome mark.

Broadcast Quality
Indicates the level of musical audio quality meeting the expectations of the television broadcast industry.

CC Controller
In MIDI terms, a continuous controller (CC) is a MIDI message capable of transmitting a range of values, usually 0-127. ... CC›s are commonly used for things like MIDI controlling volume (#7), pan (#10), data slider position (#6), mod wheel (#1) and other variable parameters.

Chorus
A distinct section in a musical composition that is repeated multiple times. The chorus compliments the other sections including the verse and bridge.

Click Book
A tool used by film composers, a click book contains tables of timings with each page in the book showing timings for one particular tempo, calibrated in film frames divided into eighths of a frame. The first click book was assembled by music editor Carroll Knudson in 1965.

Cloud Storage
Cloud storage is a cloud computing model in which data is stored on remote servers accessed from the Internet, or "cloud." It is maintained, operated and managed by a cloud storage service provider on a storage servers that are built on virtualization techniques.

GLOSSARY

Commercial Spot
The term broadcast advertising applies to commercials aired on either television or radio, which are typical called "spots". It›s also known as on-air advertising, and it›s the primary revenue generator for commercial television and radio stations.

Contract
A written or spoken agreement, especially one concerning employment, service, sales, or tenancy, that is intended to be enforceable by law.

Convolution Reverb
In audio signal processing, convolution reverb is a process used for digitally simulating the reverberation of a physical or virtual space through the use of software profiles; a piece of software (or algorithm) that creates a simulation of an audio environment.

Copyright
The exclusive legal right, given to an originator or an assignee to print, publish, perform, film, or record literary, artistic, or musical material, and to authorize others to do the same.

Counter Melody
A subordinate melody accompanying a principal one. See also *Counterpoint*.

Counterpoint
The art or technique of setting, writing, or playing a melody or melodies in conjunction with another, according to fixed rules.

Cue

Originating in theatre, a music cue is a visual or aural signal for an action to occur, either by an actor or stage hand, or for an actor to deliver a line. In production music, the piece of music being used is referred to as a 'cue'.

Cue Sheets

Cue sheets are the primary means by which performing rights organizations track the use of music in films and TV. Without cue sheets, it would be nearly impossible for such composers and publishers to be compensated for their work. An accurately filled out cue sheet is a log of all the music used in a production.

DAW

A digital audio workstation (DAW) is a computer that is specially equipped with a high-quality sound card and programming for editing and processing digital audio at a professional level. Digital audio workstations can range from a simple two-channel editor to a complete digital recording studio suite.

Dialogue

A conversation between two or more people as a feature of a book, play, or movie.

Digital Audio

In sound recording and reproduction systems, digital audio refers to a digital representation of the audio waveform for processing, storage or transmission. When analog sound waves are stored in digital form, each digital audio file can be decomposed into a series of samples.

Digital Pattern Recognition
Pattern recognition is a branch of machine learning that focuses on the recognition of patterns and regularities in data, although it is in some cases considered to be nearly synonymous with machine learning. In machine learning, pattern recognition is the assignment of a label to a given input value.

Digital Samples
A sample is a digital representation of an analog signal. Both digital video and digital audio files are created using samples.

Edit Points
A musically logical place where a music editor can cut the cue to fit within the context of the visuals.

EDM
Electronic Dance Music (EDM) is popular music intended for dancing to in clubs, typically having a repetitive beat and a synthesized backing track.

Exclusive
Restrictive agreement (involving a good, service, market, or territory) that binds a principal and an agent in an association under which neither can make any similar deals with the other's competitors (for a specified period).

Film Composer
The composer assigned to create an original piece of music to accompany a film. See also *Music Score*.

Fingerprint
Digital fingerprinting is the identification of large data files or structures

using truncated information. A fingerprinting algorithm is one that reduces a larger data set to a very small data set, sometimes called a bit string, to promote efficient identification and search protocols.

Form

Musical form (or musical architecture) refers to the overall structure or plan of a piece of music, and it describes the layout of a composition as divided into sections.

Genre

A music genre is a conventional category that identifies some pieces of music as belonging to a shared tradition or set of conventions. It is to be distinguished from musical form and musical style, although in practice these terms are sometimes used interchangeably.

Hybrid

A mixture of traditional orchestral instruments and contemporary synthesized instrument sounds.

Improvise

Musical improvisation (also known as musical extemporization) is the creative activity of immediate (*"in the moment"*) musical composition, which combines performance with communication of emotions and instrumental technique as well as spontaneous response to other musicians.

In The Box

The ability to produce music entirely within the confines of a computer without any extraneous outboard sound processing.

GLOSSARY

Instrumentation
The particular instruments used in a piece of music; the manner in which a piece is arranged for instruments.

Key Signature
Any of several combinations of sharps or flats after the clef at the beginning of each stave indicating the key of a composition.

Keyswitches
Specific notes assigned on a musical keyboard to trigger alternate sounds and articulations of a sample library instrument.

Keywords
Searchable words associated with a composition to aid in locating a desired piece of music in a music library's catalog.

KVM Switch
An acronym for "keyboard, video and mouse" is a hardware device that allows a user to control multiple computers from one or more sets of keyboards, video monitors, and mice.

Licensing
Music licensing is the licensed use of copyrighted music. Music licensing is intended to ensure that the owners of copyrights on musical works are compensated for certain uses of their work. A purchaser has limited rights to use the work without a separate agreement.

Licensing Fees
The fees associated with licensing a piece of music for public performance.

Loops

A short piece of music, often one to four measures in length, that is repeated continuously.

Magnetic Tape

A medium for magnetic recording, made of a thin, magnetizable coating on a long, narrow strip of plastic film.

Major Key

A key signature whose harmony is based on the major scale.

Master Computer

In computer networking, master/slave is a model for a communication protocol in which one device or process (known as the master) controls one or more other devices or processes (known as slaves). Once the master/slave relationship is established, the direction of control is always from the master to the slave(s).

Mastering

A form of audio post production, mastering is the process of preparing and transferring recorded audio from a source containing the final mix to a data storage device (the master); the source from which all copies will be produced (via methods such as pressing, duplication or replication).

Metadata

Metadata is "data [information] that provides information about other data." In music production, this data represents the music tracks that will be provided to a content buyer such as a television production company.

Microphone
An instrument for converting sound waves into electrical energy variations, which may then be amplified, transmitted, or recorded.

MIDI
MIDI (Musical Instrument Digital Interface) is a technical standard that describes a protocol, digital interface and connectors and allows a wide variety of electronic musical instruments, computers and other related devices to connect and communicate with one another

MIDI Keyboard
A piano-style user interface keyboard device used for sending MIDI signals or commands over a USB or MIDI cable to other devices connected and operating on the same MIDI protocol interface.

Minor Key
A key signature whose harmony is based on a minor scale. Minor scales are natural minor, melodic minor, and harmonic minor.

Mixing
The process of blending all the individual tracks in a recording to create a version of the song that sounds as good as possible – the "mix". The process can include: Balancing the levels of the tracks that have been recorded. Fine-tuning the sound of each instrument or voice using equalization (EQ)

Modulation
The process of changing from one key (tonic, or tonal center) to another. This may or may not be accompanied by a change in key signature. Modulations articulate or create the structure or form of many pieces, as well as add interest.

Mood
A temporary state of mind or feeling that occurs from hearing a particular piece of music.

Music Catalog
A collection of musical compositions is cataloged into a music catalog. The owner owns the copyrights of the cataloged compositions.

Music Composition
Musical composition can refer to an original piece of music, either a song or an instrumental music piece, the structure of a musical piece, or the process of creating or writing a new song or piece of music. People who create new compositions are called composers.

Music Cue
The common term for a piece of music that is used in a television show or film. Also referred to as 'music track'.

Music Editor
A type of sound editor in film or other multimedia productions (e.g. video or games) responsible for compiling, editing, and syncing music during the production of a soundtrack.

Music Library
Production music (also known as stock music or library music) is the name given to recorded music that can be licensed to customers for use in film, television, radio and other media. Oftentimes, the music is produced and owned by production music libraries.

GLOSSARY

Music Placements

"Placement" is the term used when your music is used in a project – i.e. "placed" in a project.

Music Score

A film score (also sometimes called background score, background music, movie soundtrack, film music or incidental music) is original music written specifically to accompany a film by a music composer.

Music Supervisor

A music supervisor is a person who combines music and visual media. According to The Guild of Music Supervisors, a music supervisor is "a qualified professional who oversees all music related aspects of film, television, advertising, video games and other existing or emerging visual media platforms as required."

Musical Palette

A sonic palette that identifies a set of musical instruments whose combination defines the sound, or "color" of the music.

Needle Drop

The term has changed its meaning over the years. The original usage is closely related to the use of "stock" or library music today. A phonograph needle being literally "dropped" onto a phonograph record (lacquer, acetate, vinyl, 78 rpm, etc.).

Networking

The exchange of information or services among individuals, groups, or institutions; specifically: the cultivation of productive relationships for employment or business

Nonexclusive

Both parties agree as to the provision of goods or services, but can also contract with other parties as to those same goods or services.

Orchestration

The arrangement or scoring of music for orchestral performance. See also *Instrumentation*.

Performance Royalties

Money earned when a musical work is performed publicly. Public performance occurs when a song is sung or played, recorded or live, on radio and television, as well as through other media such as the Internet, live concerts and programmed music services.

Phonograph Records

A sound recording consisting of a disk with a continuous groove; used to reproduce music by rotating while a phonograph needle tracks in the groove.

Plugin

An audio plug-in, in computer software, is a plug-in that can add or enhance audio-related functionality in a computer program. Such functionality may include digital signal processing or sound synthesis.

Post Production

Post-production, or postproduction, is part of the process of filmmaking, video production, and photography. It occurs in the making of motion pictures, television programs, radio programs, advertising, audio recordings, photography, and digital art. Post-production includes all stages of production occurring after shooting or recording individual program segments.

PRO

A performance rights organization (PRO), also known as a performing rights society, provides intermediary functions, particularly collection of royalties, between copyright holders and parties who wish to use copyrighted works publicly in film and television, and in locations such as shopping and dining venues.

Production Music

Production music (also known as stock music or library music) is the name given to recorded music that can be licensed to customers for use in film, television, radio and other media. Oftentimes, the music is produced and owned by production music libraries.

Public Domain

The status of a literary work or an invention whose copyright or patent has expired or that never had such protection.

Publisher

A music publisher (or publishing company) is responsible for ensuring the songwriters and composers receive payment when their compositions are used commercially.

Reality TV

Reality television is a genre of television programming that documents supposedly unscripted real-life situations, and often features an otherwise unknown cast of individuals who are typically not professional actors, although in some shows celebrities may participate. It differs from documentary television in that the focus tends to be on drama, personal conflict, and entertainment rather than educating viewers. The genre has various standard tropes, including «confessionals» (also called talking heads or interview segments) used by cast members to express their thoughts, which often double as the shows› narration. In competition-based reality shows, a notable subset, there are other common elements such as one participant being eliminated per episode, a panel of judges, and the concept of «immunity from elimination.

Recording Interface
An audio interface is a piece of hardware that expands and improves the sonic capabilities of a computer. Some audio interfaces give you the ability to connect professional microphones, instruments and other kinds of signals to a computer, and output a variety of signals as well.

Retitle
Retitling is a common practice especially among nonexclusive music libraries whereby music cues are renamed so there are no naming conflicts when registering the cues with a performance rights organization. See also *PRO*.

Reversion
In the music business, a reversion clause is part of a contract between a songwriter and a music publishing company. The clause dictates the amount of time that a publisher owns the rights to the songwriter›s work.

Royalties
Royalties are typically agreed upon as a percentage of gross or net revenues derived from the use of an asset or a fixed price per unit sold of an item of such, but there are also other modes and metrics of compensation. A royalty interest is the right to collect a stream of future royalty payments.

Royalty Free

Royalty Free Music refers to a type of music licensing that allows the purchaser to pay for the music license only once and to use the music for as long as desired.

Sample Library

A sample library is a collection of digital sound recordings, known as samples, for use by composers, arrangers, performers, and producers of music. The sound files are loaded into a sampler—either hardware or software-based—which is then used to create music.

Sample Player

A sample player ("sampler") is an electronic or digital musical instrument similar in some respects to a synthesizer, but instead of generating new sounds with filters and oscillators, it uses sound recordings (or "samples") of real instrument sounds (e.g., a piano, violin or trumpet), excerpts from recorded songs or other sounds. The samples are loaded or recorded by the user or by a manufacturer. These sounds are then played back by means of the sampler program itself, a MIDI keyboard, sequencer or another triggering device to perform or compose music. A single sample may often be pitch-shifted to different pitches to produce musical scales and chords.

Sample Rate

Sample rate is the number of samples of audio carried per second, measured in Hz or kHz (one kHz being 1 000 Hz). For example, 44 100 samples per second can be expressed as either 44 100 Hz, or 44.1 kHz. Bandwidth is the difference between the highest and lowest frequencies carried in an audio stream.

Scoring
The job of composing music to visuals, such as film and television. See also *Music Score.*

Scripted Television
A traditional form of television program where all of the story and dialogue is written ("scripted") in advance.

Section
See *Form.*

SESAC
Founded in 1930 as the Society of European Stage Authors and Composers, SESAC licenses all types of establishments and broadcast entities that use music in their business operations. Through licensing, SESAC grants copyright clearance authorization to the establishments and collects music royalties on behalf of SESAC affiliated songwriters, composers, publishers and copyright holders. See also *PRO.*

SFX
An acronym for Sound Effects. See also *Sound Effects.*

Slave Computer
see *Master Computer*

Sound Effects
A sound other than speech or music made artificially for use in a play, movie, or other broadcast production.

GLOSSARY

Sound Processing

Audio signal processing or audio processing is the intentional alteration of audio signals often through an audio effect or effects unit. As audio signals may be electronically represented in either digital or analog format, signal processing may occur in either domain.

Sound Treatment

Acoustic foam is an open celled foam used for acoustic treatment. It attenuates airborne sound waves by increasing air resistance, thus reducing the amplitude of the waves. The energy is dissipated as heat.

Soundproofing

Soundproofing is any means of reducing the sound pressure with respect to a specified sound source and receptor. There are several basic approaches to reducing sound: increasing the distance between source and receiver, using noise barriers to reflect or absorb the energy of the sound waves, using damping structures such as sound baffles, or using active anti-noise sound generators.

Stem

Stem-mixing is a method of mixing audio material based on creating groups of audio tracks and processing them separately prior to combining them into a final master mix. Stems are also sometimes referred to as sub-mixes, subgroups, or busses.

Stock Music

Production music (also known as stock music or library music) is the name given to recorded music that can be licensed to customers for use in film, television, radio and other media. Oftentimes, the music is produced and owned by production music libraries.

Structure

Song structure or the musical forms of songs in traditional music and music are typically sectional, repeating forms used in songs, such as strophic form and is a part of the songwriting process. Other common forms include thirty-two-bar form, verse-chorus form, and the twelve-bar blues.

Style

An artistic form of auditory communication incorporating instrumental or vocal tones in a structured and continuous manner.

Sync License

A music synchronization license, or "sync" for short, is a music license granted by the holder of the copyright of a particular composition, allowing the licensee to synchronize ("sync") music with some kind of visual media output (film, television shows, advertisements, video games, accompanying website music, movie trailers, etc.)

Synchronization License

See *Sync License*

Synchronized

Music that matches the events on the screen is said to be *synchronized*.

Synthesizer

An electronic musical instrument, typically operated by a keyboard, producing a wide variety of sounds by generating and combining signals of different frequencies.

Template
DAW projects utilize templates - predefined projects containing tracks already configured with instruments, plugins, and mixing settings to speed up the composing process. See also *DAW*.

Time Signature
An indication of rhythm following a clef, generally expressed as a fraction with the denominator defining the beat as a division of a whole note and the numerator giving the number of beats in each bar.

Unscripted Television
Reality television is a genre of television programming that presents purportedly unscripted dramatic or humorous situations, documents actual events, and usually features ordinary people instead of professional actors, sometimes in a contest or other situation where a prize is awarded.

Verse
In popular music, a verse roughly corresponds to a poetic stanza because it consists of rhyming lyrics most often with an AABB or ABAB rhyme scheme. When two or more sections of the song have almost identical music and different lyrics, each section is considered one verse.

Virtual Instruments
A synthesizer instrument that mimics the sound and timbre of a real instrument such as a violin or piano and is often indistinguishable from the real instrument. See also *Synthesizer*.

Wallpaper
Music that is used in a way that serves no other purpose than to have sound masking silence. The music is not supportive in any way to the visuals.

Watermark

An audio watermark is a unique electronic identifier embedded in an audio signal, typically used to identify ownership of copyright. It is similar to a watermark on a photograph. Watermarking is the process of embedding information into a signal (e.g. audio, video or pictures) in a way that is difficult to remove.

Appendix A _____

MUSIC GENRES

_____

Primary Genres

- Alternative
- Anime
- Blues
- Children's Music
- Classical
- Comedy
- Country
- Dance
  (aka EDM - Electronic Dance Music)
- Easy Listening
- Electronic
- Fitness & Workout
- Folk
- Hip-Hop / Rap
- Holiday
- Indie Pop
- Industrial
- Inspirational
  (Christian and Gospel)
- Jazz
- Latin
- Marching Band
- New Age
- Opera
- Pop
- R&B / Soul
- Reggae
- Rock
- Singer / Songwriter
- Tex-Mex / Tejano
- Vocal
- World

_____

Sub Genres

- **Alternative**
  - Art Punk
  - Alternative Rock
  - College Rock
  - Crossover Thrash
  - Crust Punk
  - Experimental Rock
  - Folk Punk
  - Goth / Gothic Rock
  - Grunge
  - Hardcore Punk
  - Hard Rock
  - Indie Rock
  - Lo-fi
  - New Wave

WRITING PRODUCTION MUSIC FOR TV

- o Progressive Rock
  (Prog Rock)
- o Punk
- o Shoegaze
- o Steampunk

- **Blues**
  - o Acoustic Blues
  - o British Blues
  - o Chicago Blues
  - o Classic Blues
  - o Contemporary Blues
  - o Country Blues
  - o Delta Blues
  - o Electric Blues
  - o Ragtime Blues

- **Children's Music**
  - o Lullabies
  - o Sing-Along
  - o Stories

- **Classical**
  - o Avant-Garde
  - o Baroque
  - o Chamber Music
  - o Chant
  - o Classical Crossover
  - o Contemporary Classical
  - o Early Music

- o Expressionist
- o High Classical
- o Impressionist
- o Medieval
- o Minimalism
- o Modern Composition
- o Opera
- o Orchestral
- o Renaissance
- o Romantic
  (early and later periods)
- o Wedding Music

- **Comedy**
  - o Dramedy
  - o Novelty
  - o Vaudeville

- **Country**
  - o Alternative Country
  - o Americana
  - o Bluegrass
  - o Contemporary Bluegrass
  - o Contemporary Country
  - o Country Folk
  - o Country Gospel
  - o Country Pop
  - o Country Rap
  - o Cowpunk
  - o Honky Tonk

o Old-Time

o Outlaw Country

o Traditional Bluegrass

o Traditional Country

o Urban Cowboy

● **Dance**
(aka EDM aka Electronic
Dance Music)

o Club / Club Dance

o Breakcore

o Breakbeat / Breakstep

o Brostep

o Chill-Out

o Chillstep

o Deep House

o Dubstep

o Electro House

o Electroswing

o Exercise

o Future Garage

o Garage

o Glitch Hop

o Glitch Pop

o Grime

o Hardcore

o Hard Dance

o Hi-NRG

o Horrorcore

o House

o Jackin' House

o Jungle / Drum'n'bass

o Liquid Dub

o Regstep

o Speedcore

o Techno

o Trance

o Trap

● **Easy Listening**

o Bop

o Lounge

o Swing

● **Electronic**

o 2-Step

o 8bit
(aka 8-bit, Bitpop and Chiptune)

o Ambient

o Bassline

o Chillwave

o Crunk

o Downtempo

o Drum & Bass

o Electro

o Electro-swing

o Electronica

o Electronic Rock

o Hardstyle

o IDM / Experimental

- Industrial
- Trip Hop

- **Folk**
  - Folk Jazz
  - Folk Metal
  - Folk Pop
  - Folk Rock
  - Folktronica
  - Freak Folk

- **Hip-Hop / Rap**
  - Alternative Rap
  - Bounce

  - Dirty South
  - East Coast Rap
  - Gangsta Rap
  - Hardcore Rap
  - Hip-Hop
  - Latin Rap
  - Old School Rap
    (Old Skool Rap)
  - Rap
  - Turntablism
  - Underground Rap
  - West Coast Rap

- **Holiday**
  - Chanukah
  - Christmas
    - Children's
    - Classic
    - Classical
    - Comedy
    - Jazz
    - Modern
    - Pop
    - R&B
    - Religious
    - Rock
  - Easter
  - Halloween
  - Thanksgiving

- **Inspirational**
  (Christian and Gospel)
  - CCM
  - Christian
    - Christian Alternative Rock
    - Christian Country
    - Christian Electronic
    - Christian Hardcore
    - Christian Hip Hop
    - Christian Metal
    - Christian Pop
    - Christian Punk

- Christian Rock
- Christian Ska
- Classic Christian
- o Contemporary Gospel
- o Gospel
- o Christian & Gospel
- o Praise & Worship
- o Qawwall
- o Southern Gospel
- o Traditional Gospel

● **Jazz**
- o Acid Jazz
- o Avant-Garde Jazz
- o Bebop
- o Big Band
- o Blue Note
- o Cabaret
- o Contemporary Jazz
- o Cool Jazz
- o Crossover Jazz
- o Dixieland
- o Ethio-jazz
- o Fusion
- o Gypsy Jazz
- o Hard Bop
- o Latin Jazz
- o Mainstream Jazz
- o Ragtime
- o Smooth Jazz

o Traditional Jazz

● **Latin**
- o Alternativo & Rock Latino
- o Argentine tango
- o Baladas y Boleros
- o Bossa Nova
- o Brazillian
- o Brown-eyed Soul
- o Cha-cha-cha
- o Contemporary Latin
- o Cumbia
- o Flamenco
- o Latin Jazz
- o Nuevo Flamenco
- o Pop Latino

- o Portuguese fado
- o Raíces
- o Reggaeton y Hip-Hop
- o Regional Mexicano
- o Salsa y Tropical

● **New Age**
- o Environmental
- o Healing
- o Meditation
- o Nature
- o Relaxation
- o Travel

- **Pop**
  - o Adult Contemporary
  - o Britpop
  - o Bubblegum Pop
  - o Chamber Pop
  - o Dance Pop
  - o Dream Pop
  - o Electro Pop
  - o Emo Pop
  - o Orchestral Pop
  - o Pop/Rock
  - o Pop Punk
  - o Power Pop
  - o Soft Rock
  - o Synthpop
  - o Teen Pop
- **R&B / Soul**
  - o Contemporary R&B
  - o Disco
  - o Doo Wop
  - o Funk
  - o Modern Soul
  - o Motown
  - o Neo-Soul
  - o Northern Soul
  - o Psychedelic Soul
  - o Quiet Storm
  - o Soul
  - o Soul Blues
  - o Southern Soul

- **Reggae**
  - o 2-Tone
  - o Dancehall
  - o Dub
  - o Roots Reggae
  - o Ska

- **Rock**
  - o Acid Rock
  - o Adult-Oriented Rock
  - o Afro Punk
  - o Adult Alternative
  - o Alternative Rock
  - o American Trad Rock
  - o Anatolian Rock
  - o Arena Rock
  - o Art Rock
  - o Blues-Rock
  - o British Invasion
  - o Cock Rock
  - o Death Metal / Black Metal
  - o Doom Metal
  - o Glam Rock
  - o Gothic Metal
  - o Grind Core
  - o Hair Metal
  - o Hard Rock
  - o Math Metal
  - o Math Rock
  - o Metal

o Metal Core

o Noise Rock

o Jam Bands

o Post Punk

o Progressive Rock (Prog Rock)

o Progressive Metal

o Psychedelic

o Rock & Roll

o Rockabilly

o Roots Rock

o Singer/Songwriter

o Southern Rock

o Spazzcore

o Stoner Metal

o Surf Rock

o Technical Death Metal

o Tex-Mex

o Time Lord Rock (Trock)

o Trash Metal

● **Singer / Songwriter**

o Alternative Folk

o Contemporary Folk

o Contemporary Singer/Songwriter

o Indie Folk

o Folk Rock

o Love Song

o New Acoustic

o Traditional Folk

● **Tex-Mex / Tejano**

o Chicano

o Classic

o Conjunto

o Conjunto Progressive

o New Mex

o Tex-Mex

● **Vocal**

o A cappella

o Barbershop

o Beatboxing

o Doo-wop

o Gregorian Chant

o Traditional Pop

o Vocal Jazz

o Vocal Pop

● **World**

o African

o Afro-Beat

o Afro-Pop

o Asia

o Australia

o Cajun

o Calypso

o Caribbean

o Carnatic

o Celtic

- Celtic Folk
- Celtic Fusion
- Celtic Hip Hop
- Celtic Metal
- Celtic Punk
- Celtic Reggae
- Celtic Rock
o Contemporary Celtic
o Coupé-décalé
o Dangdut
o Drone
o Enka
o European
o French
o French Pop
o German Folk
o German Pop
o Hawaiian
o Hindustani
o Indian Ghazal
o Indian Pop
o J-Pop

- J-Rock
- J-Synth
- J-Ska
- J-Punk
o Japanese
o Japanese Pop (aka J-Pop)
o K-Pop
o Kayokyoku
o Klezmer
o Korean Pop (aka K-Pop)
o Mbalax
o Middle Eastern
o North American
o Ode
o Piphat
o Polka
o Soca
o South African
o South American
o Traditional Celtic
o World Beat
o Zydeco

Appendix B

MOODS / FEELINGS

HAPPY / POSITIVE

Animated
Beautiful
Bold
Blissful
Brassy
Bright
Brilliant
Bubbly
Carefree
Careful
Caring
Cartoony
Cautious
Celebratory
Celestial
Cheerful
Classy
Comical
Confident
Cool
Curious
Cute
Delicate
Delighted

Determined
Easy
Ecstatic
Elated
Elegant
Enchanted
Fearful
Feel Good
Festive
Flirtatious
Fiery
Freewheeling
Friendly
Fun
Funky
Funny
Gentle
Glamorous
Glorious
Good
Good Hearted
Gorgeous
Graceful
Grand
Green
Groovy
Gutsy

Happy
Heavenly
Honest
Hopeful
Humorous
Jolly
Joyful
Light Hearted
Lifting
Loving
Magical
Majestic
Motivational
Nice
Noble
Playful
Pleasant
Pleased
Optimistic
Orange
Outgoing
Positive
Purposeful
Sassy
Shimmering
Silly
Slapstick

WRITING PRODUCTION MUSIC FOR TV

Soaring
Sparkling
Sublime
Successful
Summery
Sweeping
Sweet
Tender
Terrific
Thankful
Thrilling
Triumphant
Up
Uplifting
Vigorous
Vibrant
Whimsical
Willful
Wondrous
Yello
Zany

**SAD / BAD /
NEGATIVE**

Abrasive
Aggressive
Angry
Anguished

Anxious
Apprehensive
Awkward
Bad
Bitter
Black
Blue
Bluesy
Brooding
Chaotic
Cold
Confused
Creepy
Dangerous
Dark
Defeated
Depressed
Dirty
Disenchanted
Disillusioned
Distorted
Distressed
Disturbing
Doubtful
Down
Droning
Eerie
Evil
Forceful

Foreboding
Frantic
Freaky
Grating
Gray
Greasy
Gritty
Harsh
Haunting
Heated
Heavy
Hectic
Helpless
Hopeless
Hurt
Icy
Insanity
Irreverent
Jealous
Jumpy
Lonely
Longing
Lost
Loud
Mad
Madness
Mean
Melancholic
Melancholy

Menacing
Mischievous
Mournful
Nasty
Nervous
Obsessive
Ominous
Oppressed
Painful
Panicky
Pompous
Pounding
Pushy
Rebellious
Restless
Risque
Rowdy
Rough
Sad
Satanic
Scared
Scary
Secretive
Sinister
Snobbish
Sorry
Strange
Stubborn
Suffocating
Suggestive

Suspenseful
Sweaty
Tense
Terrified
Terror
Touch
Tragic
Unfriendly
Unraveled
Used
Vegetative
Vengeful
Vicious
Weary
Weepy
Wicked
Wild
Wistful
Worried
Wrong
Yearning

NEUTRAL

Accepting
Acoustic
Adventurous
Ambient
Ancient
Anticipation

Atmospheric
Banal
Big
Bittersweet
Bouncy
Building
Butch
Calm
Campy
Childlike
Climactic
Comforting
Crazy
Dramatic
Dreamy
Driving
Drunk
Dynamic
Edgy
Earthy
Emotional
Energetic
Epic
Erotic
Esoteric
Ethereal
Exotic
Fast
Flowing
Folksy

Free
Frisky
Futuristic
Gay
Hard
Hardcore
Heartening
Heartfelt
Heroic
Hi-Energy
Hopeful
Hot
Humble
Huge
Hypnotic
Innocent
Inquisitive
Insistent
Intense
Intricate
Intrigue
Introspective
Jerky
Jumping
Laid Back
Leftfield
Light
Live
Lively
Lofty

Luch
Martial
Mechanical
Medical
Meditative
Mellow
Melodic
Melodramatic
Metallic
Military
Moody
Moving
Mysterious
Mystical
Natural
Nostalgic
Old Fashioned
Olympic
Open
Organic
Panoramic
Passionate
Pastoral
Patriotic
Peaceful
Pensive
Percussive
Pleading
Poignant
Political

Pounding
Powerful
Prestigious
Primitive
Proud
Psychedelic
Pulsating
Punchy
Questioning
Quick
Quiet
Quintessential
Quirky
Racy
Rambling
Reflective
Regal
Relaxed
Repetitive
Retro
Reverent
Rhythmic
Risque
Rocking
Rouising
Romantic
Rootsy
Rustic
Sassy
Schmaltzy

Scientific

Sedate

Sedate

Sensitive

Sensual

Sentimental

Serene

Serious

Sexy

Simple

Sincere

Slow

Smokey

Smooth

Sneaky

Soft

Solemn

Somber

Soothing

Sophisticated

Soulful

Spacey

Sparse

Stately

Stimulating

Stirring

Street Smart

Strong

Subtle

Suggestive

Surprising

Swaggering

Sultry

Surreal

Swirling

Thinking

Thoughtful

Touching

Tranquil

Urgent

Valiant

Warm

Wholesome

Appendix C

SAMPLE LIBRARY COMPANIES

Orchestral

8Dio
www.8dio.com

AudioBro
www.audiobro.com

Big Fish Audio
www.bigfishaudio.com

Cinematic Strings
www.cinematicstrings.com

CineSamples
www.cinesamples.com

EastWest/Quantum Leap
www.soundsonline.com

Garritan
www.garritan.com

Heavyocity
www.heavyocity.com

Impact Soundworks
www.impactsoundworks.com

Miroslav Philharmonik
www.ikmultimedia.com

Native Instruments
www.native-instruments.com

Orchestral Tools
www.orchestraltools.com

Project Sam
www.projectsam.com

Spitfire Audio
www.spitfireaudio.com

Synthogy
www.synthogy.com

Vienna Symphonic Library
vsl.co.at

Vir2
www.vir2.com

Pop / Rock / Country

Chris Hein Horns
www.chrishein.net

Big Fish Audio
www.bigfishaudio.com

Garritan
www.garritan.com

Ilio
www.ilio.com

Native Instruments
www.native-instruments.com

Project Sam
www.projectsam.com

Sample Logic
www.samplelogic.com

Sample Modeling
www.samplemodeling.com

EastWest/Quantum Leap
www.soundsonline.com

Spectrasonics
www.spectrasonics.net

Vienna Symphonic Library
vsl.co.at

Vir2
www.vir2.com

Dance / Electronic / World
Heavyocity
www.heavyocity.com

Output
www.output.com

Sample Logic
www.samplelogic.com

Spectrasonics
www.spectrasonics.net

Vir2
www.vir2.com

Appendix D

COLLABORATORS' AGREEMENT
SINGLE MUSICAL WORK

This agreement is entered into for the purpose of jointly writing a musical work, "SONG", entitled "_____" We, the undersigned, agree to collaborate in writing the aforementioned songs with the following understandings:

1) We agree that no expense shall be incurred in the preparation or presentation of this song without our unanimous consent.

2) We agree that if expenses are incurred, each of the writers shall be responsible for an equal percentage of the expense.

3) We agree that the song was written in equal shares of music by each of us and we agree to divide equally any and all writer›s royalties we may receive from the sale or promotion of this song.

4) We agree that this collaboration has no effect on any collaborative efforts on other songs.

5) We agree that no changes may be made in the melody and harmony without the unanimous consent of the writers, except in the case of an imminent commercial recording where time does not allow for consultation among the writers.

6) We agree to keep each other advised of any change of address, phone number, and email address so that we can contact each other to transact any business necessary for this song. If communication sent by registered mail to a last known address is returned undeliverable, the rest of the parties can act without the knowledge or consent of the missing party/ies. Any moneys that come due to the missing party will be held in an escrow account in their name. Seven years after a

party is missing, his or her moneys will be equally divided among those who are still in contact.

7) We agree that if a dispute should arise over this agreement, we will submit it to arbitration by a lawyer of unanimous choice or by the American Arbitration Association.

8) We agree in the event of the death of one or any of the parties to this Agreement, all rights and percentages of the deceased of the composition stipulated in this Agreement shall pass to the heirs as designated in the will of the deceased. In the absence of a will, all rights of the deceased shall pass to the nearest next of kin of the deceased.

Appendix E

LIBRARY MUSIC COMPOSER AGREEMENT
EXCLUSIVE

This agreement entered into on [Month] [Day], [Year] is made between [Music Library], a California S Corporation and its assignees, designees, licensees and successors ("COMPANY") and [Composer Name] ("COMPOSER"), with respect to musical compositions and sound recordings and listed in Schedule «D» provided hereafter by COMPANY and incorporated herein by reference and made a part hereof ("COMPOSITIONS") to be included in the MUSIC LIBRARIES ("LIBRARIES").

1. Territory: The territory covered by this Agreement is worldwide and throughout the Universe.

2. Term: Except as otherwise noted in paragraphs 5 and 6, the term of this agreement is two years, corresponding to two years from the first day of the month following the date of each Schedule "D" provided to COMPOSER by COMPANY in conjunction with COMPOSITIONS submitted to COMPANY. The term will automatically renew for one year periods unless COMPANY receives email notification from COMPOSER to terminate the agreement at least 30 days prior to the initial two-year, or subsequent one-year terms.

(a) Notwithstanding termination of this agreement, COMPOSER acknowledges that COMPOSITIONS will not be excluded until the term of any existing licensing agreements between COMPANY and third parties has expired.

3. Grant of Rights: COMPOSER grants COMPANY the following irrevocable and rights with respect to the COMPOSITIONS:

(a) to record, edit, arrange, and orchestrate COMPOSITIONS, to embody those

APPENDIX E _____

COMPOSITIONS in the LIBRARIES, to make copies of such embodiments and to distribute and license such copies in all media hi perpetuity and throughout the Universe.

(b) to license the COMPOSITIONS to third parties to be recorded in synchronization or timed relation an unlimited number of times in any and all forms of media, whether now known or hereafter devised, in perpetuity and throughout the Universe.

(c) to record, use, perform, distribute and otherwise exploit the COMPOSITIONS or any portions thereof for the purpose of advertising, publicizing, or otherwise promoting any productions which incorporate in whole or in part the COMPOSITIONS and the exhibitors thereof by any means without limitation in any medium of forum now known or hereafter devised.

(d) to re-title, or re-name COMPOSITIONS, and or register COMPOSITIONS with applicable Performing Rights Organizations with COMPOSER as Writer and COMPANY as Publisher.

4. Representations and Warranties: COMPOSER warrants, represents, and covenants that:

(a) COMPOSER has the full right, power, and authority to make this Agreement and to grant the rights granted herein.

(b) Any and all material written or furnished by COMPOSER hereunder is or will be original with COMPOSER, and shall not infringe upon or violate the right of privacy of, or constitute a libel, slander or unfair competition against, or violate any common law right, copyright or any other right of any person or entity.

WRITING PRODUCTION MUSIC FOR TV

(c) The services of COMPOSER and the Music (COMPOSITIONS) and the Masters are not subject to any union collective bargaining agreement and COMPOSER shall not have any rights or privileges (nor COMPANY any obligations) as specified in any union or collective bargaining agreement and COMPOSER shall be solely responsible for obtaining any and all required licenses, permissions and consents from third parties that may be required in connection with COMPANY's exercise of the rights granted to COMPANY herein including, without limitation, the COMPOSITIONS.

(d) There are no liens, claims or encumbrances which might conflict with or otherwise affect any of the provisions of this Agreement or COMPANY's promotion or exploitation of the COMPOSITIONS in any and all media whether now known or hereafter devised, throughout the universe, in perpetuity.

(e) COMPOSITIONS are exclusive to COMPANY for the term of this agreement, and are not now nor will they be represented by any other production music library or third party service. COMPOSER reserves the right to use COMPOSITIONS in his own production work so long as they do not do so through creation of or in association with another production music library

(f) COMPANY shall not be required to pay monies to or otherwise compensate COMPOSER for any reason, including but not limited to the licensing, mechanical, synchronization, and or any other income that may be accrued by COMPANY resulting from the licensing, exploitation, and distribution of COMPOSITIONS embodied in the LIBRARIES.

(g) COMPANY is under no obligation to include COMPOSITIONS in the LIBRARIES.

5. Publisher's Performance Royalties: COMPANY shall be entitled to one-

hundred percent (100%) of all performing rights fees and royalties payable to publishers (100% of the so called "publisher›s share") in conjunction with or as a result of the performance of any part of the COMPOSITIONS as re-titled in the Music Library in perpetuity.

6. Writer›s Performance Royalties: COMPOSER shall be entitled to one-hundred percent (100%) of all performing rights fees and royalties payable to writers (100% of the so called "writer's share") in conjunction with or as a result of the performance of any part of the COMPOSITIONS as re-titled in the Music Library in perpetuity.

7. Indemnity: COMPOSER shall indemnify and hold harmless COMPANY and COMPANY's employees and its officers, agents, designees, successors, assigns and licensees from and against any and all liabilities, claims, costs, damages, and expenses (including attorneys› fees and disbursements) arising out of or in connection with a breach or alleged breach of the covenants, warranties and representations contained in this Agreement.

8. Any controversy or claim arising out of or relating to this agreement, or the breach thereof, shall first be the subject of good faith negotiations between the parties to resolve the dispute. If the dispute cannot be settled by good faith negotiation between the parties within thirty (30) business days from the date the dispute first arose, the dispute shall be settled by binding arbitration conducted in the county of Los Angeles, California, and administered by JAMS in accordance with its streamlined arbitration rules and procedures or subsequent versions thereof (the "JAMS Rules"), and judgment rendered by the arbitrator(s) may be entered in any court having jurisdiction thereof. This Agreement shall be binding upon and inure to the benefit of the parties› respective heirs, successors, licensees, transferees and assigns.

9. COMPANY and COMPOSER agree that this Agreement may be executed in multiple counterparts with the counterparts being taken together as one original. Additionally, facsimile signatures, scanned, and PDF documents shall be binding, the same as an original.

Appendix F

LIBRARY MUSIC COMPOSER AGREEMENT
EXCLUSIVE

This AGREEMENT is made and entered into as of the [Month] [Day], [Year], by and between [Music Library], LLC, located at [Business Address] (hereinafter referred to as "Company") and [Your Name] and [Mailing Address] (hereinafter referred to as "Composer").

For and in consideration of the mutual covenants herein set forth, the parties do hereby agree as follows:

1. Composer's Affiliation: Composer is a member of or affiliated with the following performing rights society: ASCAP

2. Engagement: (a) Company hereby specifically commissions Composer to render their services as writers, Composer, arrangers, orchestrators and producers under the direction, control and supervision of Company in connection with the creation of musical works and masters for use in, without limitation, audio-visual works. Composer shall compose, record, produce and deliver to Company masters (the "Masters") embodying one or more musical works (the "Compositions. Each of the Compositions and Masters is set forth in Schedule "A" hereto. The Masters were delivered on CD. Each party to this agreement agrees that they have received good and valuable consideration, and that they are freely entering into this agreement upon each of the conditions and terms, which are set forth herein. (b) Company may, from time to time; commission Composer to render additional services in connection with the composition and delivery of additional musical works and masters. All such services, music works, and masters shall be subject to the terms and conditions set forth herein, as modified by Company. All such musical works and masters shall be set forth in successive addenda to Schedule "A" (i.e. Schedule A-1, Schedule A-2, etc.). Each such additional schedule shall

set forth the number of musical works and masters to be delivered to Company, a deadline date for the delivery of such musical works and masters, the musical style and duration(s) of such musical works and masters, the amount of the advance or fee (if any) to be paid, and the format in which each of the musical works and masters shall be delivered. Company shall be under no obligation to accept delivery of any such musical works and masters unless and until Company approves the same.

3. Term: See 4c.

4. Company's Rights: (a) Subject to the terms hereof, Composer hereby irrevocably and absolutely grant to Company, its successors and assigns, exclusively, One Hundred (100%) percent of the so-called "publisher's share" and retain the "writer's share". Composer hereby grants, transfers, conveys and assigns directly to Company one-hundred (100%) percent of the, right, title and interest throughout the universe, including, without limitation, one-hundred (100%) percent of the copyright, the right to secure copyright registration and any and all copyright renewal rights, in and to the Compositions and Masters. Composer shall upon Company's request, cause to be executed and delivered to Company any transfers of ownership of copyrights (and all renewal and extensions) in the Compositions and Masters and any other documents, including any separate agreement and/ or assignment of copyright in Company's customary form with respect to each Composition and Master, including, without limitation, the "Assignment Letter" in the form attached hereto and marked as Schedule "B", as Company may deem necessary or appropriate to vest in Company the rights granted to Company in this Agreement. If Composer fail to execute any such transfer, document, agreement or assignment, Company is hereby appointed Composer' attorney in fact to execute such transfer, document, agreement or assignment. The failure of either of the parties hereto to execute any such transfer, document, agreement or assignment shall not affect the rights of each of the parties hereunder, including,

but not limited to, the rights of Company to all of the Compositions and Masters.

(b) Subject to the terms hereof, Composer acknowledges that included, without limitation, within the rights and interest hereinabove referred to is Composer' irrevocable grant to Company of the following rights:

(i) To perform the Compositions and Masters for profit or otherwise by means of public and private performance, radio broadcasting, television, or by any and all other means, whether now known or which may hereafter come into existence.

(ii) To alter, edit, add to, subtract from, adapt, arrange, rearrange, revise, re-record, translate, retitle and otherwise modify the Compositions and Masters, in whole or in part in any and all media. Composer hereby waives any claim that Composer may have under any doctrine of "moral right" or any other similar doctrine, existing under the law of any country which may be now or hereafter recognized.

(iii) To add new lyrics to the music of the Compositions or new music to the lyrics of the Compositions or to add lyrics to the Compositions in instrumental form.

(iv) To secure copyright registration and protection of the Compositions and Masters, one-hundred (100%) percent in the Company's, as author thereof at Company's own cost, expense and at Company's election, including any and all renewals and extensions of copyrights.

(v) To make or cause to be made and to license others to make, and to distribute, phonorecords, tapes, compact discs, and any other reproductions of the Compositions and Masters in whole or in part, or of any element thereof in such form or manner and as frequently as Company in its sole and uncontrolled discretion shall determine, and the right to manufacture, advertise, license or sell such reproductions for any and all purposes, whether now known or which may hereafter come into existence.

(vi) To print, publish, sell, display, advertise, copy, record, exhibit, reproduce, reprint, distribute and use, and to license others to do any or all of the same, the Compositions and Masters, or any portion thereof, in any and all forms, whether now known or which may hereafter come into existence, for any purpose.

(vii) To use and publish and to permit others to use and publish Composer' name (including any professional names heretofore or hereafter adopted by Composer), likenesses or photographs and biographical materials in connection with the use, advertising and exploitation of the Compositions and Masters. Composer shall not authorize or permit the use of their names or likenesses or biographical materials concerning them for or in connection with the Compositions and Masters, other than by or for Company; provided, that Composer may make references to the Compositions and Masters and Composer' engagement hereunder in connection with personal publicity (including demo material) regarding Composer.

(viii)   To synchronize, or grant licenses to others to synchronize, the Compositions and Masters with sound motion pictures, television, video and other audio-visual devices, whether now known or which may hereafter come into existence.

(ix) To exploit any and all other rights of every kind and any nature now or hereafter existing under and by virtue of any common law and/or statutory rights including, without limitation, any copyrights, renewals and extensions thereof in any and all of the Compositions and Masters and/or parts and elements thereof.

(c) Company reserves the right to determine, at its sole discretion, the manner, extent and means of exploiting the Compositions and Masters. Notwithstanding the foregoing, Company shall not be obligated to exploit the Compositions and Masters. However, should the Compositions not be used in a broadcast performance medium within five years from the date of this agreement all rights will revert back to Composer. This contract will automatically extend for an additional five years unless either party notifies the other party in writing 90 days before the end of the term of this contract that they wish to discontinue the agreement. Company will, however, retain the non-exclusive right, in accordance with the terms of this agreement, after the five year initial period has expired should the composition not be used in a performance medium.

5. Compensation: Provided that Composer shall faithfully and completely perform the material terms, covenants and conditions of this Agreement, Company hereby agrees to pay Composer for the services to be rendered by Composer under this Agreement, and for the rights acquired hereunder, the following compensation based on the Compositions and Masters which are subject hereof:

(a) Company agrees to exploit the compositions in order to obtain future royalty payments from the aforementioned performance rights society.

(b) Composer shall receive one hundred (100%) percent of the so-called «writer›s share» of public performance royalties throughout the world directly from Composer' own affiliated performing rights societies. Composer shall have no claim whatsoever against Company for any royalties received by Company from any performing rights society, which makes payment directly to writers and Composer. However, if (and to the extent that) any such society is precluded in the future (by legislation, court decree, or otherwise) from licensing performing rights for any type of use for which such society currently licenses performing rights, and collecting fees or royalties therefor, or Company elects to license such rights directly, Company shall have the right to license directly the public performance rights in the Compositions to third parties and collect both the «writer›s share» and "publisher's share" of performance income directly and Company shall pay to Composer fifty percent (50%) of all such sums which are received by Company. Such monies shall be separately distributed at the same time as statements are otherwise due pursuant to the terms of this Agreement. Notwithstanding the foregoing, Company shall not be obligated or required to collect any fees in connection with any license of performance rights. Composer further agrees that Composer will become affiliated with a performance rights society within three

(3) months of the signing of this Agreement if Composer is not currently so affiliated. Composer shall not be entitled to receive any share of the so-called "publisher's share" of public performance royalties.

(c) Royalties as hereinabove specified shall be payable solely to Composer in instances where Composer is the sole writer of the entire Composition(s), including the words and music thereof. However, in the event that one or more other songwriters, Composer and/or lyricists are writers together with Composer of any Composition (including persons employed by Company to add, change or translate the words or to revise or change the music), then the foregoing royalties shall be divided equally among Composer and such other persons.

(d) Composer agree and acknowledges that Company shall have the right to withhold from the royalties payable to the Composer hereunder such amount, if any, as may be required under the applicable provisions of any law or other governmental regulation or code, and Composer agrees to execute such forms and other documents as may be required in connection therewith. Monies shall only be due hereunder after being received by Company in the United States and will be paid at the same rate of exchange as Company is paid. All monies received from foreign sources shall be reduced by applicable foreign taxes it being agreed that Composer is an independent contractor.

(e) In no event shall Composer be entitled to share in any advance payments, guarantee payments or minimum royalty payments which Company shall receive in connection with any subpublishing agreement, collection agreement, licensing agreement, recording agreement, distribution agreement or other agreement covering the Compositions and/or Masters. Except as otherwise provided herein, no other royalties or monies shall be paid to Composer.

(f) Composer shall receive fifty percent (50%) of any and all net sums actually received (less costs paid or incurred) by Company in the World in connection with any Non-Broadcast License (as defined below) of any or all of the Compositions and Masters. Notwithstanding the foregoing, such percentage shall be pro-rated in connection with any blanket-use Non-Broadcast License (i.e., a license granting use of a Library [as defined below] of musical works for non-broadcast purposes in connection with a single production [e.g., a single audio-visual production]) by multiplying the same by a fraction, the numerator of which is the total number of musical Compositions contained in such Library and the denominator of which is the total number of musical works contained in such Library.

(g) Composer shall receive thirty-three percent (33%) of any and all net sums actually received (less costs paid or incurred) by Company in the World in connection with any All Rights Theatrical licenses (as defined below) of any or all of the Compositions and Masters.

(h) In no event shall Composer be entitled to greater than fifty percent (50%), subject to proration hereunder, of any and all net sums received in connection with any single license granted hereunder. The phrase «costs paid or incurred» shall be inclusive of any fees or other consideration payable to any sub-licensee, sub-publisher and/or any other third party in connection with the exploitation and administration of the Composition and Masters.

(i) Composer shall receive fifty percent (50%) of any and all net sums actually received (less costs paid or incurred*) by Company from the exploitation by Company of mechanical rights in the Compositions and Masters in connection with the commercial sale of phonorecords (i.e., sound only recordings, excluding CD ROM's) embodying the Compositions and/or Masters. (*Note: costs connected with the recording and production of the masters and costs connected with the manufacture of compact discs embodying the Masters shall not be included as "costs paid or incurred".)

6. Composer' Credit: Conditioned upon Composer' full and faithful performance of all of the terms and conditions hereof, Company shall accord a credit to Composer in the liner notes of all CDs (compact discs) and CD ROM's embodying the Compositions and Masters, or any of them, which are manufactured and distributed by Company. All characteristics of such credit shall be at Company›s sole discretion. The casual or inadvertent failure by Company to comply with the foregoing credit provision shall not constitute a breach of this Agreement.

7. Warranties, Representation, Covenants and Agreements: Composer hereby warrant and represent that Composer has the full right and authority to enter into and perform this and all claims, rights and obligations whatsoever; all the results and proceeds of the services of the Composer hereunder, and all of the titles, lyrics and music and other contributions to the Compositions and masters and each and every part and element thereof, are and shall be new and original (or based on material in the public domain, if so requested by Company) and capable of copyright protection throughout the entire world, and that no part or element thereof shall infringe upon any other material, or shall violate or infringe upon any common law or statutory rights of any party.

8. Definitions:

(a) "Compositions" will mean any musical work, including titles, lyrics, if any, libretto, music, musical scores and all arrangements (including public domain arrangements), adaptations, translations and other version thereof and all other words derived from the foregoing, including all interpretations regardless of duration. Different arrangements, adaptations, translations, recordings or other version of a musical work will be considered, collectively, on Composition. A Composition that would otherwise be a Composition will not be deemed a Composition unless it is acceptable to Company, as commercially satisfactory, in Company›s sole discretion.

(b) "Masters" will mean every form of recording but not limited to, a compact disc, digital audio tape, analog audio tape, or any other contrivance, appliance or device whatsoever, whether not know, developed or discovered at anytime hereafter, bearing or used for emitting or transmitting sound derived from recordings of the Compositions, whether or not the same also bears or can bear visual images. Each of the Masters must be commercially and technically suitable, in Company's sole discretion.

(c) "Non-Broadcast License" will mean a per use ("needledrop") synchronization license that is granted for a non-broadcast media only, including corporate/industrial music uses, theatrical exhibition (trailer and in-film use), home video trailer, and non-broadcast production for sale (i.e., audio cassettes, video cassettes, computer software and CD ROM's).

(d) "All Rights Theatrical License" will mean a per use («needledrop») synchronization license that is granted for a theatrical motion picture or a theatrical motion picture trailer when such license is granted worldwide in perpetuity for all media including, but not limited to, broadcast (i.e., free TV, cable TV, pay TV, radio), non-broadcast, theatrical exhibition and home video.

(e) "Library" will mean a collection of two or more musical works and› or recordings of such musical works.

(f) "CD ROM" will mean a compact disc interactive software embodying a multi-media software program for simultaneous interactive presentation of video, audio, graphics, text and data.

9. Accounting: Company will compute the total royalties earned by Composer pursuant to this Agreement within sixty (60) days after the six (6) month period ending the preceding December 31, and within sixty (60) days after the six (6) month period ending the preceding June 30, and will submit to Composer the royalty statement for each such period together with the net amount of such royalties, if any, which shall be payable. All statements shall be binding upon Composer and not subject to any objection by Composer for any reason unless specific written objection, stating the basis thereof, is submitted by Composer

to Company within one (1) year from the date such statement is due or would have been due if required. Composer shall be precluded from maintaining any actions, claims or proceedings against Company with respect to any statement or accounting or absence of statement or accounting unless such action, claim or proceeding is commenced against Company in a court of competent jurisdiction within one (1) year after the date such specific written objection is submitted to Company as provided for herein.

10. Indemnification: Composer agree and does hereby indemnify, save and hold Company harmless from any and all loss and damage (including actual attorneys› fees) arising out of or connected with any claim, action or demand by a third party which is inconsistent with any of the warranties, representation, covenants or agreements made by Composer in this Agreement, and time with respect to any liability or claim to which the foregoing indemnity applies. Pending the determination of any such claim, demand or action, Company may withhold payment of any or all royalties or other monies payable hereunder.

11. Notices: Any written notices which Company shall desire to give to Composer hereunder, and all statement and payments which shall be due to Composer hereunder shall be addressed to Composer at the addresses set forth in page 1 hereof until Composer shall give Company written notice of new addresses. All notices shall be served by mail, postage prepaid, addressed as aforesaid. The date of making personal service or of mailing or of depositing in a telegraph office, whichever shall be first, shall be deemed the date of service.

12. Modification, Waiver, Illegality: This Agreement may not be canceled, altered, modified, amended or waived, in whole or in part, in any way, except by an instrument in writing signed by both Company and Composer. The waiver by either party of any breach of this Agreement by the other party in any one or more instances shall in no way be construed as a waiver by such party of any subsequent

APPENDIX F _____

breach (whether or not of a similar nature) of this Agreement by the other party. If any part of this Agreement shall be held void, invalid or unenforceable, it shall not affect the validity of the balance of this Agreement. This Agreement shall be governed by and construed under the laws and judicial decisions of the State of North Carolina.

13. Assignment: Company shall have the right to assign this Agreement or any of its rights hereunder to any person, firm or corporation. This Agreement shall inure to the benefit of and be binding upon each of the parties hereto and their respective successors, assigns, heirs, executors, administrators and legal and personal representatives. Composer may not assign or transfer any of Composer' (or Company›s) rights or obligations under this Agreement and any attempted assignment or transfer shall be void; provided, that Composer may assign their right to any monies payable hereunder with prior written notice to Company.

14. Headings: The headings of paragraphs or other divisions hereof are inserted only for the purpose of convenient reference. Such headings shall not be deemed to govern, limit, modify or in any other manner affect the scope, meaning or intent of the provisions of this Agreement or any part thereof, nor shall they otherwise be given any legal effect.

15. Entire Agreement: This Agreement supersedes any and all prior negotiation, understandings and agreements between the parties hereto including, without limitation, any prior publishing agreements, with respect to the subject matter hereof. Each of the parties acknowledges and agrees that neither party has made any representation or promises in connection with this Agreement nor the subject matter hereof not contained herein.
IN WITNESS WHEREOF, the parties hereto have executed this Agreement as of the day and year first written.

WRITING PRODUCTION MUSIC FOR TV

Appendix G

LIBRARY MUSIC COMPOSER AGREEMENT
NON-EXCLUSIVE

AGREEMENT between [Music Library], [Business Address] ("COMPANY") and the person(s) and/or entity(s) named as licensor on the Signature Page of this Agreement as well as any additional people and/or entities named in Attachment 1 (together and separately, "Licensor") This Agreement is made as of the date set forth on the Signature Page. The person and/or entity listed on the Signature Page, shall also be referenced in this Agreement as the "Rights Manager."

WHEREAS, Licensor solely owns and controls certain musical compositions (lyrics and musical notes), along with sound recordings embodying those compositions (musical compositions and sound recordings together, hereafter "Compositions"), all as itemized on the attached Music Information Sheet attached as Exhibit A and incorporated herein by this reference,

WHEREAS, Licensor wishes to permit COMPANY, on a non-exclusive basis, to make those Compositions available for use by third parties for exploitation in all media and distribution channels now known or hereafter devised at COMPANY's sole discretion, pursuant to licenses to be granted by COMPANY on Licensor›s behalf, and in exchange for compensation to be paid by such licensees for each such permitted use ("Permitted Use"); and

WHEREAS, Licensor wishes to authorize COMPANY to market, advertise and promote the Compositions in all media now known or hereafter devised, and to administer and collect all revenues earned in connection with any such licensing by COMPANY and to exercise such other rights as may be necessary to accomplish the foregoing.

NOW, THEREFORE, in consideration of the mutual covenants and undertakings herein contained, it is hereby agreed by the parties hereto as follows:

1. Rights Granted.

(a) Licensor hereby grants to COMPANY the non-exclusive right, privilege and license, during the Term of this Agreement, and throughout the Territory:
• to permit third parties to audition, via the Internet or otherwise, the Compositions, and to provide copies of the Compositions to third parties via digital transmission or other pre-recorded format, or any other medium now known or hereafter devised; and/or
• to grant to such third parties (hereinafter "Third Party Users") all rights COMPANY deems necessary to use the Compositions (in whole or in part and to edit, loop and re-mix Compositions) for use in all media now known or hereafter devised including but not limited to, television and film, radio, internet, computer (including all forms of PDAs), The rights granted herein shall include, but not be limited to: a) all rights needed to synchronize and edit the Compositions, or parts of the Compositions, to motion and/or still images and to re-mix, re-edit, loop and re-master the Compositions; and b) the rights to use the Compositions in all non-commercial and commercial ways including, but not limited to, in advertising of products and promotion of programming; c) all rights to use the Compositions as an independent work or to incorporate the Compositions into the work of another (audio, visual or both); d) all rights to create and maintain (and/or to allow authorized third parties to create and maintain), for purposes of tracking and/or content protection purposes, so-called "audio fingerprints" and/or watermarks of the Compositions; and, in addition e) all rights to create derivative works that are not already specified above. Notwithstanding any other provision herein, the term of any license issued by COMPANY hereunder to any Third-Party User may be for any period of time, whether in perpetuity and/or for any shorter period of time, as shall be determined and negotiated from time to time by COMPANY in its sole discretion.

(b) Also notwithstanding anything to the contrary contained in this Agreement, COMPANY shall be under no obligation to make every all or any Compositions provided by Licensor available for audition and use by Third-Party Users, it being understood and agreed that COMPANY shall also be entitled, in its sole discretion, to select particular Compositions to be made available to Third Party Users. Despite any other provision herein to the contrary. COMPANY shall not issue any exclusive license(s) to any Third-Party Users without Rights Manager's consent.

2. Term.

(a) The term of this Agreement (the "Term") shall commence upon the parties' mutual execution of this Agreement and shall then continue for an initial term ("Initial Term") of two (2) years. Upon expiration of the Initial Term, the Agreement shall then continue on a year by year basis, provided, however, that either party may avoid any further extension(s) of this Agreement by giving the other party written notice of termination ("Notice of Termination") at least sixty (60) days prior to end of the Initial Term, or after the expiration of the Initial Term at least sixty (60) days prior to the beginning of the next contract year. Notwithstanding the foregoing and any other provision herein, if the Term would otherwise expire prior to the last day of a calendar quarter, the final contract year shall, for the purpose of simplifying the administration of royalties hereunder, be deemed to continue until the end of that calendar quarter. By way of illustration, if this Agreement is entered into on May 25, 2009, and one of the parties gives the other party a notice of termination at least sixty (60) days prior to May 25, 2011, then in such event the Term of this Agreement shall expire on June 30, 2011 (the last day of the calendar quarter in which May 25 occurs).

(b) Upon the expiration or the Term of this Agreement, COMPANY shall no longer have the right to issue any new licenses to any Third-Party Users for any

APPENDIX G _____

new Permitted Use.

(c) However, notwithstanding anything herein, the terms of Third Party license agreements shall not be affected by termination of this Agreement any other provision herein, and/or any act or inaction of the parties to this Agreement. COMPANY shall have the right to continue to administer and collect the Gross Receipts earned from the Permitted Use of the Compositions, in accordance with the terms of the applicable license(s) pertaining to the Permitted Use, and for the full term thereof, and such rights of COMPANY and such Third-Party Users shall not be affected or terminated in any way by any termination of this Agreement or by any Notice of Termination hereunder. Artist agrees that in the event of a dispute arising out of this Agreement, Artist's sole remedy shall be for money damages and in no event shall Artist seek an injunction in connection with the use of Compositions herein.

3. Territory. The territory (the "Territory") subject to the grant of rights provided for in this Agreement shall be the universe.

4. COMPANY's Right to Administer.

(a) During the Term hereof, COMPANY shall have the rights:
• to administer and permit the exploitation of Licensor's entire interest in the Compositions for any Permitted Use, throughout the universe (and/or any part thereof);
• to publish, use and license the Compositions for any use by any Third Party User, including, but not limited to, the following licenses: electrical transcription, synchronization, videogram, commercial synchronization, musical product, publicity rights,, print, electronic print, performance, multimedia, digital transcription and reproduction (which shall include, but not be limited to, stream, download, edit, re-mix, loop and synchronize). For the purpose of clarification,

and not as a limitation of COMPANY's rights herein, all licenses listed herein shall apply to all media and channels of distribution currently known and all media and forms of distribution devised in the future.

• to execute in Licensor's name or stead any license and agreements affecting the Compositions in connection with any Permitted Use, as defined below,

• to collect all Gross Receipts payable to COMPANY earned by and derived from the Compositions pursuant to or as a result of any Permitted Use;

• to file title registrations with any performance rights organization(s) (for example, without limitation, ASCAP or BMI), assigning a new and specific title, in COMPANY's discretion, for any Compositions hereunder, in order to be able to more accurately track the performance rights income hereunder, provided, however, that COMPANY shall not be obligated to do so in any instance; and/or

• to assign in the normal course of business or license such rights to third parties, subject to the terms and conditions set forth herein.

(b) The term "Gross Receipts" is hereby defined as any revenue derived from the Compositions paid by the Third-Party User for the related Compositions, less any amounts paid to or deducted by foreign subpublishers, sublicensees, agents, collection agencies and local performing and mechanical rights societies. The term "Gross Receipts" shall also include, without limitation, mechanical royalties, synchronization fees, print income and the so-called "Publisher's Share" (as that term is customarily used in the music industry) of all public performance income resulting from the Permitted Uses in respect of the Compositions. For purposes of clarification, COMPANY shall not be entitled to any share of the so-called "Writer's Share" of any such public performance income.

5. No Guarantee of Use or Compensation. While COMPANY anticipates a strong and broad demand for the musical material it will make available, and has agreed to make available the musical material provided by Licensor based on the quality of the material presented, COMPANY will be licensing musical material

from other sources in addition to Licensor, which materials will or may be of both a similar and different musical style and character from that provided by Licensor. COMPANY cannot predict or guarantee the types of music that Third-Party Users will be interested in licensing, and COMPANY makes no representation or guarantee as to the number of uses (if any) of any Compositions, and/or the amount of compensation (if any) which will become payable to Rights Manager as the result of Licensor entering into this Agreement.

6. Allocation of Gross Receipts Received from Third Parties.

(a) The following provisions of this sub-paragraph 6(a) shall apply to all Gross Receipts::
• For its services hereunder, COMPANY shall retain and be paid fifty percent (50%) of the Gross Receipts derived from all Permitted Uses hereunder, for the life of the subject use. Rights Manager shall be paid by COMPANY Fifty percent (50%) of the Gross Receipts received by COMPANY as a result of all Permitted Uses hereunder for the life of the subject use. COMPANY shall not be responsible for the payment of any third party payments, including (but not limited to) royalties to third party songwriters, performers, and producers, and Rights Manager shall be solely responsible for such payments.

(b) At Rights Manager's request, COMPANY shall provide Rights Manager with a copy of any licenses issued by COMPANY to third parties for Compositions that are specifically requested by Rights Manager.

(c) Also for purposes of clarification, if and to the extent that COMPANY receives advances from third parties in connection with the licensing of its entire catalog or the material of multiple licensors, Licensor shall not be entitled to any share of such advance, due to the difficulty of determining the specific and actual future usages and income to which such advances would apply. Despite the foregoing, however, if and when a royalty is thereafter generated in such instances from (and is specifically attributable to) such use of Licensor's material, then in such event the Licensor's royalty account hereunder will be promptly credited with Licensor's share of such royalty.

7. Statements and Payments to Licensor.

(a) COMPANY shall maintain true and complete books and records concerning all Gross Receipts and all payments due to Licensor hereunder. COMPANY shall compute and pay royalties due to Licensor hereunder on a calendar quarterly basis within sixty (60) days following March 31, June 30, September 30, and December 31, respectively, in each case with respect to the Gross Receipts hereunder in connection with monies actually received by COMPANY during the immediately preceding three (3) month period in connection with any Permitted Uses, such payments to be accompanied by a statement setting forth the source of such royalties. COMPANY shall be under no obligation to render any statement or make any payment until such time as accumulated royalties due Licensor hereunder equal or exceed Twenty-five Dollars ($25.00). COMPANY shall have the right to deduct or withhold income taxes and similar taxes from sums payable to Licensor hereunder pursuant to the laws of the relevant territory, provided that COMPANY shall, when readily available, furnish to Rights Manager, with each statement, any necessary information which shall enable Licensor, upon presentation of such, to endeavor to obtain income tax credit from the United States Internal Revenue Service for any taxes so withheld.

(b) For any payment due to Rights Manager hereunder and the individuals comprising Licensor, COMPANY shall be entitled to make a single payment made payable to Rights Manager, who shall in turn be responsible for allocating and paying to each of the individuals comprising Licensor the sum due to each such individual.

APPENDIX G

8. Audit Rights. At any time within two (2) years after any royalty statement is rendered to Rights Manager hereunder, Rights Manager shall have the right to give COMPANY written notice of Rights Manager's intention to examine COMPANY's books and records with respect to such statement. Such examination shall be commenced and completed within three (3) months after the date of such notice, at Rights Manager's sole cost and expense, by any certified public accountant or attorney designated by Rights Manager, provided he or she (or any member or associate of the firm within which he or she is affiliated) is not then engaged in an outstanding examination of COMPANY's books and records on behalf of a person or entity other than Rights Manager. Such examination shall be made during COMPANY's usual business hours at the place where COMPANY maintains the books and records which relate to Rights Manager and which are necessary to verify the accuracy of the statement or statements specified in Rights Manager's notice to COMPANY and the examination shall be limited to the foregoing. In the event that any audit undertaken by the Rights Manager shows that COMPANY has understated the amount payable to the Rights Manager by more than ten per cent (10%) or $500 USD, whichever is the greater, for any calendar year, COMPANY will reimburse the Rights Manager, in addition to the amount due, the reasonable costs of such audit. Such payment shall be made within thirty (30) working days of receipt by Licensee of the results of such audit. Licensor's right to inspect COMPANY's books and records shall be only as set forth in this Paragraph 8 and COMPANY shall have no obligation to produce such books and records more than once with respect to each statement rendered to Licensor.

9. Promotional Use by COMPANY. COMPANY and its licensees shall be entitled to use and/or duplicate the Compositions in connection with auditioning of Compositions, and/or to electronically transfer or transmit the Compositions for promotional purposes, in any manner or media now known or hereafter discovered, including (but not limited to) in connection with an audition of all or

a part of any Compositions to any Third-Party User, all without any payment to Licensor, Rights Manager or any third party.

10. Delivery. Within ten (10) days of the date of execution of this Agreement, Rights Manager shall deliver to COMPANY, at Rights Manager's sole expense and to the address and as otherwise directed by COMPANY, a copy of each Licensed Compositions/Master Recording identified on the Music Information Sheet, such copy to be in 16 bit, 44.1khz audio CD format, or such other audiophile format as may become available in the recording industry and requested by COMPANY. Said copies of such Compositions shall become the sole property of COMPANY and COMPANY shall be under no obligation to return said copies to Licensor at any time, including (without limitation) upon the termination or expiration of this Agreement. However, upon termination or expiration of this Agreement, said copies will be destroyed.

12. Retention of Ownership in Compositions. Except as expressly set forth in this Agreement, nothing contained herein shall be deemed to convey to COMPANY or any Third-Party User or any other designee, assignee or licensee of COMPANY any ownership (such as, for example, any copyright ownership) of any Compositions hereunder.

13. Rights to Names and Likenesses. Licensor hereby grants to COMPANY the non-exclusive right to use and the right to permit others to use the names, likenesses of and biographical materials concerning all who contributed to the Compositions (including, but not limited to, composers, recording artists, producers, and technicians), for advertising and trade purposes in connection with the use and exploitation of the Compositions as set forth in this Agreement and/ or COMPANY.

14. Credits for Licensor. COMPANY will instruct and use reasonable efforts to

cause any Third-Party User of one or more Compositions, to the extent possible, to include in the materials incorporating the such Compositions a credit identifying the writers and performers of the applicable Compositions, provided, however, that, despite the foregoing, each member of Licensor and each signatory hereto acknowledges and agrees that they may not receive such credit.

15. Warranties and Representations of Licensor & Rights Manager.

(a) Licensor, and each member of Licensor, and each signatory comprising Licensor hereunder, hereby warrants and represents that: • they are under no disability, restriction or prohibition, whether contractual or otherwise, with respect to (i) their right to enter into this Agreement, and (ii) their right to grant the rights granted to COMPANY hereunder;
• COMPANY shall not be required to make any payment of any nature for, or in connection with, the acquisition, exercise or exploitation of rights by COMPANY pursuant to this Agreement, except as expressly and specifically provided herein;
• Neither the "Materials" nor any use of the Materials by COMPANY or any Third- Party User will violate or infringe upon any common law or statutory rights of any third party, including, without limitation, any contractual rights, copyrights, trademarks, right not to be defamed and rights of privacy.
* Neither Licensor nor any member of Licensor shall enter into any agreement which would interfere with or prohibit the exercise by COMPANY or any Third-Party Users of any of the rights granted hereunder; and
• Neither Licensor nor any member of Licensor shall communicate with any Third-Party User or any of its agents, including advertising agencies, in connection with any Permitted Use hereunder of any Compositions.

(b) Rights Manager, in addition to the representations and warranties above in Section 15 (a) hereby represents and warrants that:
* No Person other than Licensor or members of Licensor or Persons who are

signatory parties to this Agreement has or have any right, title or interest, including copyright, in or to the Compositions;

• Compositions provided to COMPANY hereunder identified on the Music Information Sheet are original to Licensor, and no Person (other than one (1) or more members of the undersigned Licensor) wrote, or owns or controls, any of the Compositions. ("Materials" means any musical (including, but not limited to, lyrics, notes, and sound recordings), artistic and literary materials, ideas, bios, photographs, likeness, artwork, trademarks, logos, graphics and other intellectual properties, furnished or selected by Licensor and/or contained in the Compositions);

• All of Licensor's and the members of Licensor's and signatory Persons' representations and warranties are true and correct as of the execution date of this Agreement and shall be true upon delivery of Compositions subject to this Agreement and shall remain true at all times during any Permitted Use hereunder;

16. Indemnity. Licensor and Rights Manager (jointly and separately, Indemnitors) will at all times indemnify and hold harmless COMPANY and each and every Third-Party User of Compositions from and against any and all claims, damages, liabilities, costs and expenses, including, but not limited to, legal expenses and reasonable counsel fees, arising out of any alleged breach or breach by Licensor of any warranty, representation or agreement, express or implied, made by Licensor herein which results in a final non-appealable judgment by a court of competent jurisdiction or is settled with Rights Manager's prior written consent, which consent shall be neither unreasonably withheld or delayed. Indemnitors will reimburse COMPANY and/or Third Party User on demand for any payment made at any time in respect of which COMPANY or Third-Party User is indemnified hereunder. Without limiting any of its other rights or remedies, upon the making or filing of any claim, action or demand arising out of any such alleged breach or breach by Licensor, COMPANY shall be entitled to withhold from any amounts payable under this Agreement such amounts as are reasonably related to

the amount of the action, claim or demand, plus estimated counsel fees and costs pending the final disposition of such action, claim or demand. Rights Manager shall be notified of any such claim, action or demand and shall have the right, at Indemnitor's own expense, to participate in the defense thereof with counsel of Indemnitor's own choosing; provided, however, that COMPANY's decision in connection with the defense or settlement of any such claim, action or demand shall be final.

17. Assignment. This Agreement shall not be assignable by either party hereto during the Term, except that COMPANY may assign this Agreement to a corporation or other entity of which a majority interest is then owned, or which is then controlled, by COMPANY, or which succeeds to COMPANY's interests; and Licensor may assign this Agreement to any corporation or other entity of which a majority interest is then owned, or which is then controlled, by Licensor.

18. Definitions. As used in this Agreement, the following terms shall have the meanings set forth below: (a) "Compositions" - all single musical composition, irrespective of length, including all spoken words, lyrics, score, notes, performance, sound recording and bridging passages and including a medley, written and/or performed by one (1) or more members of Licensor, listed in Music Information Sheet; (b) "Permitted Use" - the particular use or form of exploitation of such Compositions by a third party pursuant to a license granted by COMPANY hereunder; (c) "Master Recording" or "Master" - each recording of sound, by any method and on any substance or material, embodying a performance by one (1) or more members of Licensor, of a Composition identified on the Music Information Sheet attached hereto and provided to COMPANY pursuant to this Agreement; (d) "Person" and "Party" - any individual, corporation, partnership, association or other organized group of persons or legal successors or representatives of the foregoing; (e) "Records," "Phonograph Records" and "Recordings" - all forms of reproductions, whether now known or hereafter devised; (f) "Notice of Termination"

- a written notice from Licensor to COMPANY notifying COMPANY that this Agreement is to be terminated pursuant to paragraph 2 above.

19. Notices. All notices hereunder shall be in writing and shall be sent by registered mail or certified mail, return receipt requested, postage prepaid and with receipt acknowledged, or by hand (to an officer if the party to be served is a corporation), or by facsimile or e-mail, all charges prepaid, at the respective addresses set forth above, or on the Signature Page, or such other address or addresses as may, from time to time, be designated in writing by either party; provided, that royalty payments may be made by means of regular mail. The date of making of personal service or of mailing or of transmission via facsimile, or transmission via e-mail, whichever shall be first, shall be deemed the date of service, except that notice of change of address shall be effective only from the date of its actual receipt.

20. General Provisions. A waiver by either party of any term or condition of this Agreement in any instance shall not be deemed or construed as a waiver of such term or condition for the future, or of any subsequent breach thereof. All remedies, rights, undertakings, obligations and agreements contained in this Agreement shall be cumulative and none of them shall be in limitation of any other remedy, right, undertaking, obligation or agreement of either party. In the event that any one or more of the provisions of this Agreement shall be held to be invalid, illegal or unenforceable, the validity, legality and enforceability of the remaining provisions shall not in any way be affected or impaired thereby. Moreover, if one or more of the provisions contained in this Agreement shall be held to be excessively broad as to duration, scope, activity or subject, such provisions shall be construed by limiting and reducing them so as to be enforceable to the maximum extent allowed by applicable law.

21. Governing Law. This Agreement shall be deemed entered into in the State of Washington, and the validity, interpretation and legal effect of this Agreement

shall be governed by the laws of the State of Washington applicable to contracts entered into and performed entirely within the State of Washington, with respect to the determination of any claim, dispute or disagreement which may arise out of the interpretation, performance, or breach of this Agreement. The parties agree that any action, suit or proceeding based upon any matter, claim or controversy arising hereunder or relating hereto shall be brought solely in the State courts or the Federal Court of King County, State of Washington. The parties hereto consent to (and irrevocably waive any objection to) the venue and jurisdiction of the above-mentioned courts, including any claim that such action, suit or proceeding has been brought in an inconvenient forum. Any process in any action or proceeding commenced in the courts of the State of Washington, or elsewhere arising out of any such claim, dispute or disagreement may, among other methods, be served upon Rights Manager or COMPANY by delivering or mailing the same via registered or certified mail, addressed to Rights Manager or COMPANY, as the case may be, at the address first above written or such other address as Rights Manager or COMPANY may designate. Any such delivery or mail service shall be deemed to have the same force and effect as personal service within the State of Washington or the jurisdiction in which such action or proceeding may be commenced.

22. Right to Cure Breach. In no event shall COMPANY be deemed at any time to be in breach of any obligation hereunder, unless and until Rights Manager shall have first given COMPANY written notice of such breach, by certified or registered mail, return receipt requested and received, describing in detail the breach, and COMPANY then fails to cure that breach within (30) days of its receipt of such notice. Licensor remedies under this Agreement shall be limited to money damages and in no instance shall Licensor seek equitable relief including, but not limited to, any injunctive relief against the exploitation of the Compositions.

23 Paragraph Headings. Paragraph headings used herein are for convenience only, and shall not affect the interpretation of this Agreement.

24. Legal Representation. Each party acknowledges and agrees that they have been represented by independent legal counsel or have had the unrestricted opportunity to be represented by independent legal counsel of their own choice for purposes of being advised in connection with the negotiation and execution of this Agreement.

25. Entire Agreement. This Agreement (including Exhibit A and Attachment 1), contains the entire understanding of the parties hereto relating to the subject matter hereof and cannot, subject to Paragraph 2 above, be changed or terminated except by an instrument signed by Rights Manager and an officer of COMPANY.

Appendix H _____

RECOMMENDED READING

CREATIVE
On the Track: A Guide to Contemporary Film Scoring
by Fred Karlin and Rayburn Wright

On Writing: A Memoir of The Craft
by Stephen King

MOTIVATION
The Compound Effect
by Darren Hardy

The War of Art
by Steven Pressfield

The Artist's Way
by Julia Cameron

Creating a Life Worth Living
by Carol Lloyd

Art & Fear: Observations on the Perils (and Rewards) of Artmaking
By David Bayles & Ted Orland

MARKETING
Purple Cow: Transform Your Business by Being Remarkable
by Seth Godin

Show Your Work!: 10 Ways to Share Your Creativity and Get Discovered
by Austin Kleon

BUSINESS & NETWORKING
The Go-Giver, Expanded Edition: A Little Story About a Powerful Business Idea
by Bob Burg and John David Mann

The 10X Rule: The Only Difference Between Success and Failure
by Grant Cardone

Eat That Frog!: 21 Great Ways to Stop Procrastinating and Get More Done in
Less Time
by Brian Tracy

Acknowledgements   _____

To begin with, I need to say thanks to my publisher, Ron Middlebrook, for making this book possible. Ron had been after me for years to write a book. After finally wearing me down, here it is. Ron has been a good friend and his encouragement has been instrumental in making this happen.

A special thanks to all of the interviewees for their time and candidness: Talented composers Matt Hirt, Lydia Ashton, and Tracey & Vance Marino - I'm honored to call you my friends. For their valuable insight into music libraries, Jeff Rona (Liquid Cinema) and Edwina Travis-Chin (APM Music). Jeff is also an amazing composer in his own right, plus his Orbit and Eclipse sound libraries are amazing! A big thanks to music supervisor Jen Malone for fitting me into her very busy schedule; and last but not least, thanks to music attorney Erin M. Jacobson (themusicindustrylawyer. com) for her detailed insights into contracts.

Thank you, Kevin Kiner, for not only writing the foreword to this book but for also taking the time to listen to my music all those years ago and inviting me to participate in writing cues for some of the shows you were working on. You opened the doors for me. I guess that makes me "lucky".

Thanks to Tim Perry at Arqen Acoustics (arqen.com) for use of their studio diagram.

I would be remiss not to mention Michael Laskow (Taxi A&R). Michael has championed the advancement of production music composers for over 20 years and his educational podcasts, videos, and music conferences were certainly an inspiration for writing this book. Thanks to everyone in the LATC hang, in particular, Kevin Mathie and Paula McMath. Everybody in the group has influenced and improved my knowledge of the production music business.

Finally, a big thanks to my wife, Leanne, for holding down the fort while I burned out from multiple concurrent projects.

About the Author

Steve Barden is a production music composer for film and television. His music can be heard on television somewhere in the world on a daily basis. His music has aired on ABC, CBS, NBC, FOX, ABC Family, A&E, American Heroes Channel, Animal Planet, Biography Channel, Bravo, The Cooking Channel, Discovery Channel, E!, Food Network, Game Show Network, HGTV, Investigation Discovery, Lifetime, MTV, National Geographic Channel, Oprah Winfrey Network, Outdoor Channel, Oxygen, PBS, Science Channel, Style Channel, SyFy Channel, TLC, Travel Channel, truTV, Univision, and VH1.

Steve is multi-instrumentalist playing guitar, piano, and currently learning the violin. He has studied guitar at the Guitar Institute of Technology in Hollywood (currently Musician's Institute) and studied film scoring at UCLA. He has scored animated television series Tic Tac Toons, Journey to the Heart of the World, and Button Nose. He also scored the award winning animated short, The Baseball Card Shop, originally

produced by Nickelodeon. He has also written jingles and theme songs for Los Angeles radio personalities, Mark & Brian, and also Kevin & Bean.

Steve is a husband, father, grandfather, and cat guardian. He lives in Lakewood, California with his wife, Leanne, and an undisclosed number of cats.

A, A♯/B♭, B, C, C♯/D♭, D, D♯/E♭, E, F, F♯/G♭, G, G♯/A♭

At CENTERSTREAM Publishing we've got these arranged in way that can make you cry, burn, shred, giggle, love, hate, explore, wonde ponder, and understand. It's astonishing what those 17 little notes can d

In Dave Celentano's hands he shreds them, Ken Perlman's banjo woun them into melodic songs. Joe Weidluch's guitar twisted them into jaz patterns. Brian Emmel's bass slapped them into shape, Jorge Polanuer sax put them into classic songs, Tom Ball's harmonica blew them into ol familiar patterns, Max Palermo's bass exercises made them the ultimate Ron Middlebrook turned them into a best seller, Kenny Sultan's guitar pt them in the blues, and Glen Caruba pounded his drums into new groove with them. Find out what these little notes have done for others and ca do for you, send for your Centerstream catalog today.

P.O. Box 17878
Anaheim Hills, CA 92817
centerstrm@aol.com
www.centerstream-usa.com